THE GREAT WICKET-KEEPERS

THE GREAT
WICKET-KEEPERS

David Lemmon

Stanley Paul

London Melbourne Sydney Auckland Johannesburg

FOR VAL
Some small thanks for all
those lost Sundays when I was
trying to imitate John Murray

Stanley Paul & Co. Ltd

An imprint of the Hutchinson Publishing Group

17–21 Conway Street, London W1P 6JD

Hutchinson Publishing Group (Australia) Pty Ltd
PO Box 496, 16–22 Church Street, Hawthorne, Melbourne, Victoria 3122

Hutchinson Group (NZ) Ltd
32–34 View Road, PO Box 40–086, Glenfield, Auckland 10

Hutchinson Group (SA) Pty Ltd
PO Box 337, Bergvlei 2012, South Africa

First published 1984
© David Lemmon 1984

Set in Linotron Baskerville by
Input Typesetting Ltd, London

Printed and bound in Great Britain by
Anchor Brendon Ltd, Tiptree, Essex

British Library Cataloguing in Publication Data

Lemmon, David
  The great wicket-keepers.
  1. Cricket – Wicket-keeping – Biography
  I. Title
  796.35′824′0922   GV915.A1
        ISBN 0 09 155210 9

Contents

Preface   7
1   Introduction   9
2   The Pioneers   15
3   Blackham: the 'Prince of Wicket-keepers'   23
4   'Dick' Lilley: a Model of Consistency   32
5   'Tiger' Smith: a Much-loved Man   43
6   Strudwick: Record Breaker and Gentleman   53
7   Oldfield and the Australian Tradition   63
8   George Duckworth and the Cult of Personalities   73
9   Les Ames: the Great All-rounder   80
10   'Jock' Cameron and the South Africans   92
11   Don Tallon: Master Craftsman   99
12   The Australian Heritage: Langley and Grout   106
13   The Golden Age of Godfrey Evans   113
14   Murray and Parks: the Great Debate   122
15   Alan Knott: a Fine Example   136
16   Bob Taylor: the Last of the Purists   143
17   'Old Iron Gloves': Rodney Marsh   151
18   Wasim Bari and the Commonwealth Tradition   157
19   In the Shadow of Engineer: Syed Kirmani   162
20   Conclusion   166
Leading Wicket-keepers and Their Records   168
Index   172

Preface

A book of this nature is not possible without the help and consideration of many people. In particular, I would like to thank those who gave so freely of their time to talk to me, and others who wrote to me. I would like to give special thanks to Les Ames, Howard Levett, John Murray, Wasim Bari, Syed Kirmani, Bob Taylor, Eifion Jones, David East, Bobby Parks, Paul Downton and Jack Richards, not only for speaking to me, but for the pleasure that they have given me.

PHOTOGRAPHIC ACKNOWLEDGEMENTS

For permission to reproduce copyright photographs, the publishers would like to thank Sport & General Press Agency Ltd, Press Association Photos, Adrian Murrell/All-Sport, Ken Kelly, Central Press Photos Ltd, BBC Hulton Picture Library and All-Sport Photographic

1

Introduction

'Personally, I should like to see the wicket-keeper more handsomely rewarded than he is,' wrote A. E. Knight in 1906, 'and I would infringe upon the delightful social communism of our fees to the extent of awarding him an extra sovereign in every match.'

Albert Ernest Knight was not a wicket-keeper, but he was a thinking cricketer who wrote one of the very best books about the game, *The Complete Cricketer*. He played for Leicestershire and three times for England, and was a Methodist lay preacher who would pray before he went out to bat and often, it was complained, invoke the help of the Almighty when he was at the wicket.

Whatever the opinions might have been as to his soliciting extra aid when batting, few people would have disagreed with his assessment of the importance of the wicket-keeper. He was only echoing a view that Ranjitsinhji had expressed some six years earlier, and, indeed, that John Nyren and Robert Allan Fitzgerald had voiced in the sixty years before Ranjitsinhji wrote his *Jubilee Book of Cricket*.

Nor did the estimate of the wicket-keeper's importance in the side die with Knight and the Prince. The MCC coaching manuals continue to advise that the best wicket-keeper must be selected irrespective of all other considerations for, through his expertise, he can decide the course of a match. Unfortunately, it seems that many British selectors do not read the MCC coaching manuals, for, in the past decade, the art of wicket-keeping has been demeaned, and selections made which have treated with contempt the artistry of some of the great performers behind the stumps.

Roger Tolchard, a wicket-keeper of modest accomplishment and a batsman of above-average ability, was selected for an England tour in front of wicket-keepers with greater claims, and as a result we lost a wicket-keeper-selector, John Murray. Bairstow, Downton and, more recently, Ian Gould, all likeable young men, have been preferred to the great Bob Taylor because, it was supposed, they could scramble more runs when batting at number eight in one-day cricket.

One wonders what Ranji, Knight and the rest would have thought, for wicket-keeping is an art and the skilful wicket-keeper is an artist. Like all artists, he must suffer, for his gift is innate and not fully comprehended by many of those who watch. He is regarded with a mixture of awe and distrust because of the passion that he often displays for his work, and most of the time he is simply taken for granted because he fulfils duties that, because he so obviously loves them, others feel must be easy and natural. It is like looking at any work of art. Only the composure of the finished product is seen. The agony of creation remains hidden. The wayward line where inspiration has failed is visible to all, but not the hours of endeavour.

Passion, love, innate ability – these are strong words to use of a position on the field in a summer game; but they are the ones applicable. Certainly they come easily from the lips of William Howard Vincent 'Hopper' Levett, a very fine wicket-keeper, one of the game's great characters and, at the age of seventy-four, still a great thinker on the art of wicket-keeping and an adviser to young men who eagerly seek his help.

It was as a very young boy at his preparatory school that 'Hopper' Levett first became intrigued by wicket-keeping. He liked the feel of a ball and he would practise for hours, taking the ball and catching, before he ever played in a real match. He would go down to the boot room and there, with the aid of an old tip-up desk and the gutta-percha inside of a golf ball, he would learn how to be a wicket-keeper.

He would throw the ball on to the wall so that it would bound back off the lid of the desk, and he would catch it at whatever angle it came off. Sometimes it would miss the desk and hit the rear wall and this presented an extra difficulty, but he would keep at it for hours, fascinated by the art of wicket-keeping.

The first occasion he ever remembers stumping a victim in a match occurred when he was eight years old. He was keeping wicket for his preparatory school against the Fathers' Eleven at Linden Park, Tunbridge Wells, in Kent. Levett senior came in to face a bowler named Maidwell who, by preparatory-school standards, was rather quick. Levett junior was standing up to Maidwell, as he was to do to all but the very quickest bowlers throughout his career, and he missed the first ball bowled to his father. The second ball fizzed off the pitch and beat Levett senior's forward stroke; as he lifted his heel, he was eagerly stumped by his son. 'I was eight years old,' says 'Hopper', 'and it is the first stumping I can ever remember making. It still gives me pleasure today.'

Wicket-keeping continued to absorb him. When he watched Kent in 1919 he never took his eyes from Jack Hubble.

He believes fervently that wicket-keeping cannot be taught, that it is a God-given gift, and that a wicket-keeper will prosper with good eyesight and quickness of brain. Terence Prittie, and any who have studied the game, would support this view: 'Stumping requires, above all, speed of hand and eye. Speed of foot is complementary but subsidiary. For, generally speaking, the first-class batsman leaves his ground for so short a time that it is barely possible to stump him off the widish ball, which requires more than the movement of a single foot to reach.'

What Levett does insist, however, is that one wicket-keeper can pass on the benefit of his experience to others. He can mention points to young players, but he must always qualify his advice with the warning that what he is advising suited himself, but it may not suit anyone else and should be rejected if it does not satisfy.

The most important thing is to take every ball whatever happens. It does not matter if it hits the bat or the pad; the wicket-keeper must be taking it in his mind and body all the time. The biggest sin a wicket-keeper can commit is to surrender the ball.

There are times, of course, when the keeper will miss the ball and even miss a chance, but he must never let it bother him, Levett insists; he'll make up for it, and if he worries about it, he'll meet more disaster.

It was a good job that Levett himself did not worry, for in his first match for Kent, against Worcestershire at Tunbridge Wells in 1930, he dropped Fox, the Worcestershire opener off 'Tich' Freeman. Fox went forward and edged the ball; it hit Levett's gloves and he dropped it. 'I had followed it,' he remembers, 'instead of going with it, and it went down. At the end of the over, as we crossed, "Tich" said to me, "Young man, if you do that sort of thing, you won't stay long in this game." But I don't think it does to start too well. You can only get better.'

Training remained a joy to him. He continued to practise for hours, throwing a ball against a wall and moving along with it. He always used a golf ball and if he missed the ball as it came back off the wall, he would punish himself by adding twelve more catches to his session. Not that it really was punishment:

There is joy in everything you do as a wicket-keeper. It is lovely being there. I saw the best batsmen in the world, Sutcliffe, Hobbs, Bradman, from a closer view than anybody else ever had. It was a joy to see them get runs. I had a lot of fun, but one thing I always tell a youngster is: 'never let the umpire down'. I had many catches and stumpings given not out, but I never argued. The best umpires are those who make the least mistakes.

In Levett's day the good wicket-keeper influenced a side. He only stood back when he was driven back. He was someone for the crowd to look at, not a showman, but certainly an accomplished artist. He worked on the

12

batsmen who were bred to move their feet to the pitch of the ball. In the thirties, the batsmen danced.

The bowlers tried to outguess the batsmen. It was a good-humoured contest. 'I always treated every bowler with great respect when I was keeping wicket,' says Levett. 'I insisted that they all gave me difficulty. You had to watch them. In that way, I kept my concentration. I could always read "Tich's" googly, but I never took it for granted.'

The game, of course, has changed considerably since the end of the Second World War. The fielding today is more agile than it was before the war and, indeed, for a good few years afterwards, and wicket-keepers are far more acrobatic.

In the thirties there were gentlemen on both sides who enjoyed a good lunch and were rather lethargic in the afternoon. The game is now more professional, and financial considerations have brought a totally different attitude to the sport. One wonders if the following story about 'Hopper' Levett could be told of anyone today.

Evidently, he had enjoyed a rather good night on the evening before a match, and he is said to have stood totally motionless as the first ball of the day flashed past him for 4 byes. The next delivery was touched down the leg-side by the batsman, and Levett, flinging himself, caught it and got up, saying gleefully, 'Not bad for the first ball of the morning, eh?'

The diving catch was not characteristic of the age. Before the war, the position of first slip was renowned, and there were fielders there who had won great reputations for their catching ability – men like Hammond, Woolley and John Langridge. It was not expected that the wicket-keeper should get in their light. Today's vogue is for a keeper like Alan Knott to poach to off and leg, but then nowadays even the best wicket-keepers spend most of their time standing back.

Brian Johnston, perhaps the most enthusiastic wicket-keeper never to have played first-class cricket, remembers that at school a master noticed that he had a tendency to move backwards – in a sense, to run away from the ball.

The master took Johnston to a fives court where he set up a wicket and placed Johnston behind it and in front of a board which prevented him from moving back. Then he bowled at him, and after a couple of hours each day for a few weeks, the fault was cured.

Today so much of the time is spent standing back that one wonders if such a practice would be thought of. 'The wicket-keeper today,' complained one old professional, 'is a slip with gloves on, but the outstanding one is the one who can do his stuff to slow bowling.'

Certainly, most wicket-keepers get their deepest satisfaction from keeping to a spin bowler, for it is he who tests the intelligence and reflexes as well as the concentration. Johnston remembers keeping to Richie Benaud in a charity match and waiting eagerly for the chance of a stumping. It did not come. The batsman charged down the wicket at Benaud, missed, and was stranded in mid-wicket; but the ball had turned so sharply and so quickly that Johnston, too, missed the leg-break, and the chance was gone. 'It wasn't just the leg-breaks off Richie, either,' said Johnston. 'I missed one off Jim Laker. It is amazing how sharply those chaps could turn a ball, and no warning that I could see.'

At least Johnston's misses were in charity matches where nobody was too worried about the result. Eifion Jones, on the other hand, for over twenty years Glamorgan's wicket-keeper, remembers dropping Geoffrey Boycott off the first ball of the day. It was a straightforward out-swinger from Malcolm Nash: 'Geoff hung his bat out and got a touch. Everybody went up and the ball went straight into my gloves and out again. At the end of the day he was somewhere close to two hundred. It was the only time in all the years that I've played against him that he's ever bought me a drink.'

2

The Pioneers

The recent demeaning of the wicket-keeper's art is, perhaps, a reversion to the prehistoric ages of cricket when no special member of the side was designated to the task. It was customary for the bowler to act as stopper when he was not bowling, but he did not stand close to the wicket, wore no protection, and stumpings were rare and never recorded as such in the scores.

By the middle of the eighteenth century, however, the position of wicket-keeper was certainly established. Hanging in the Cricket Memorial Gallery at Lord's is an oil painting entitled *The Game of Cricket as played on the Artillery Ground, London, 1743.* The artist was Francis Hayman, RA, and the scene he depicted is of an underarm bowler, the two-stump wicket, and a rather casual array of fielders. Crouched behind the wicket in an uncomfortable-looking stance is a bald-headed man who bears a striking resemblance to William Hogarth, the great social satirist and a friend of Hayman's. His left knee is bent and close to the ground, his right leg is in front of the left, and the hands are in an awkward snap-like position as if about to clap. Obviously, it is his job to stop the balls that the batsman misses.

The posture of this wicket-keeper is more modern than one would expect of the period, but then it is doubtful how accurately the picture mirrors cricket of the time. For example, one is uncertain as to the function of the two gentlemen at square-leg. Is one a fielder and one an umpire, and are they having a chat? Or are they simply two gentlemen out for a stroll, oblivious of the fact that

15

there is a cricket match in progress and that they are walking across the pitch, a phenomenon not uncommon today?

There is certainly a nonchalance about the whole field, and the scorer, at silly point, would need a crash helmet in today's game.

The wicket-keeper, however, is eager and alert, no doubt anticipating John Nyren's instruction in *The Young Cricketer's Tutor* nearly a century later:

The wicket-keeper holds the most important station of all the fieldsmen, and for the following reasons. He always presides at that wicket from which the ball is struck. This very circumstance will enable him to command a full view of the whole field with greater facility than any other player. His position, being just behind the batsman, is another reason why his situation is the best to move the fieldsmen. He therefore is the General, and is deputed to direct all the movements of the fieldsmen; not, however, by word of command, like the military commander, but by the simple motion of his hand; and the reason for this will be obvious to every one; for instead of calling out to each fieldsman distinctly, and by so doing putting the striker upon his guard, the alteration and exact position of each fieldsman is effected in perfect silence. This motion of the hand cannot, of course, be executed with effect, without the proper attention on the part of the fieldsmen; each one, therefore, upon arriving at his appointed place, should turn his eyes towards the wicket-keeper, to discover if he be satisfied with his exact position.

The question of silence had been touched upon by the Mary-Le-Bone Club in their revised Laws of Cricket in 1830, but with instructions not to disturb the batsman:

The wicket-keeper must remain quietly at a reasonable space behind the wicket, and not stir till the bowler has delivered the ball. If any portion of his body, limbs, or head be beyond, or even over the wicket, the batter shall not be considered out, although the ball hit the wicket. The wicket-keeper also is not allowed to annoy the striker, either by noise, uncalled-for remarks, or unnecessary action.

It is apparent that by the beginning of the nineteenth century the influence of the wicket-keeper upon the course of the game had become a significant one.

Perhaps the legislators were mindful of the behaviour of William Yalden, wicket-keeper for Surrey and England in their matches against Hambledon and Kent in the second half of the eighteenth century, who was accused of acts of 'low cunning, as is not consistent with the character of an Englishman'.

Yalden, born in 1739, was a thin, dark-looking man of some 5 feet 10 inches. He was reputed to be an agile wicket-keeper who once jumped over a fence and fell flat on his back while taking a catch. His main claim to fame was his keeping to the shooters of 'Lumpy' Stevens, with whom he worked on the Earl of Tankerville's estate.

Yalden was brought up on the rough wickets of the eighteenth century and the two-stump wicket, and it was the bowling of his colleague 'Lumpy' Stevens which led to the introduction of the third stump.

On 22 May 1775 a match was played in the Artillery Ground between five of Hambledon and five of All England. When Hambledon's last man, John Small, went to the wicket 14 runs were needed, and he got them. It was noticed, however, that three of Stevens's deliveries had passed between the two stumps, and it was felt to be hard on the bowler that his straightest balls should be penalized; so the following year the third stump was introduced.

Yalden was to play cricket for nearly another twenty years and live to be eighty-four; but if he were the first wicket-keeper to win renown, it was not without controversy. 'His word,' says Nyren, 'was not always to be depended on when he had put a man out – he would now and then shuffle, and resort to trick.'

No such accusation was ever made against Tom Sueter, a builder and carpenter of Hambledon, who subsequently played for Surrey until about 1791. He brought from John Nyren the most lyrical of praise:

About this time, 1778, I became a sort of farmer's pony to my native club of Hambledon, and I never had cause to repent the

17

work I was put to; I gained by it that various knowledge of the game which I leave in the hands of those who knew me in my 'high and palmy state' to speak to and appreciate. This trifling preliminary being settled, the name and figure of TOM SUETER first comes across me – a Hambledon man, and of the club. What a handful of steel-hearted soldiers are in an important pass, such was Tom in keeping the wicket. Nothing went by him; and for coolness and nerve in this trying and responsible post, I never saw his equal. As a proof of his quickness and skill, I have numberless times seen him stump a man out with Brett's tremendous bowling. Add to this valuable accomplishment, he was one of the manliest and most graceful of hitters. Few would cut a ball harder at the point of the bat, and he was, moreover, an excellent short runner. He had an eye like an eagle – rapid and comprehensive. He was the first who departed from the custom of the old players before him, who deemed it a heresy to leave the crease for the ball; he would get at it, and hit it straight off and straight on; and, egad! it went as if it had been fired. As by the rules of our club, at the trial-matches no man was allowed to get more than thirty runs, he generally gained his number earlier than any of them. I have seldom seen a handsomer man than Tom Sueter, who measured about five feet ten. As if, too, Dame Nature wished to show at his birth a specimen of her prodigality, she gave him so amiable a disposition, that he was the pet of all the neighbourhood: so honourable a heart, that his word was never questioned by the gentlemen who associated with him: and a voice, which for sweetness, power and purity of tone (a tenor), would with proper cultivation, have made him a handsome fortune. With what rapture have I hung upon his notes when he has given us a hunting song in the club-room after the day's practice was over!

In this passage, the first eulogy on a wicket-keeper, John Nyren says that nothing went by Sueter, but this is contradicted by the fact that an invaluable member of the Hambledon side was Sueter's companion, George Leer – Little George, the long-stop.

The long-stop formed an essential partnership with the wicket-keeper, who did not take upon himself to stop every ball. The deeds of Sueter and Leer were recorded in rhyme:

I had almost forgot, they deserve a large bumper;
Little George, the long-stop, and Tom Sueter, the stumper.

Yalden had had Quiddington as his long-stop, and it was
to be some years before the position was dispensed with.
   Nyren saw John Hammond of Pulborough, Sussex, as
the only rival to Sueter as a wicket-keeper: 'Both of them
would put the wicket down without any flourishing or
fuss; but I never saw either of them do so without a
chance of putting out the batsman. The young wicket-
keeper will do well to follow their example.'
   Hammond prospered as batsmen became more adven-
turous and advanced down the wicket to hit the bowling.
He played for the Players in the first two matches against
the Gentlemen at Lord's in 1806. He caught the Hon. E.
Bligh and stumped Lambert, the top scorer, in the first
match, and in the second he stumped John Willes in
both innings and bowled Lord Frederick Beauclerk in the
second, for he often turned his hand to bowling, too. As
Nyren played against him in these matches, his praise of
Hammond is obviously based upon keen observation.
   The quickness in stumping had now become all-
important, and between 1829 and 1846 the wicket-keeper
for the Players was Edward Gower Wenman of Kent.
He stood without pads or gloves, his eyes rooted to the
batsman's feet, ready to break the wicket and glance at
the umpire in appeal if he had the slightest chance of
a stumping, and so good was his judgement that his
supplication was rarely refused.
   Wenman stood 6 feet tall, weighed 15 stone, and was
a wheelwright and carpenter by trade. Writing in 1846,
when Wenman was forty-three years old, W. Denison said
of him in his *Sketches of the Players*:

Few men who have appeared on the cricket field have gained
and maintained a more universal feeling of respect and esteem
for themselves than has the subject of this sketch. His quiet
and respectful demeanour to all, and the care he has invariably
taken to cheer up a young candidate for fame, especially, where,
for the time he may have been unfortunate, in addition to his
great qualifications as a cricketer, have tended to this end.

Wenman was considered to have no equal as a wicket-keeper, particularly as he had to keep wicket to the fierce bowling of Alfred Mynn. Denison was astonished that he had lasted so long, for it was known that he had sustained punishment of the most painful character on many occasions, 'whilst his hands have been severely cut about as no other hands have been, unless the party may have stood against Mr Mynn, or Brown of Brighton, when he was in his zenith'.

The battering that Wenman and others received was due not only to the lack of protection, but also to the fact that they stood up to quick bowling on wickets which were very far from flat. The stance was much more upright than it is today, and the wicket-keeper invariably took the ball one-handed so that the left hand was as important as the right in pulling off stumpings.

So invaluable was Wenman to the great Kent side of the first half of the nineteenth century that when it was learned that he would not captain the side in the match against England at Lord's in 1840, bets were placed against the Kent side. When he did play in the first match in 1841, Kent won by 2 wickets and, according to the Rev. James Pycroft, Wenman stumped three men, 'one of them . . . off Mynn's swift bowling – happy for Kent that Mynn had any wicket-keeper to do him justice'.

Wenman was not only a fine batsman and wicket-keeper, but also a very good bowler. In the Gentlemen *v.* Players match of 1829, when the Gentlemen played with twelve men and were allowed the services of Lillywhite and Broadbridge, who won the match for them, Wenman took the wickets of Budd, Jenner and Potter in the second innings.

Herbert Jenner, later Jenner-Fust, was the Gentlemen's wicket-keeper in that match and had four dismissals as the Players were bowled out for 24 and 37. Jenner was a remarkable cricketer, who first played for the Gentlemen in 1827. He could bowl, bat and keep wicket, and it was his bowling, together with that of G. T. Knight, who is also credited with a stumping, that won the match for the Gentlemen by 29 runs.

In 1833 he was president of MCC. He was twenty-seven years old at the time, and he was the last man to play in the Gentlemen *v*. Players match while president of the club.

He was instrumental, along with Charles Wordsworth, in starting the annual fixture between the universities of Oxford and Cambridge. In the inaugural fixture at Lord's in 1827 play was restricted to one day, 4 June, by bad weather. Wordsworth captained the Oxford side, who scored 258, and Jenner led the Cambridge side, scoring 47 of their 92 runs, bowling at one end and keeping wicket at the other.

He did not captain the next match, in 1829, but bowled three and stumped three. After 1836 he virtually ceased to play cricket, but by then he had established himself as one of the great wicket-keepers. Denison saw him as without parallel in that he had an astonishing facility not merely of bringing his left hand into effective play, but of taking and covering balls on the leg-side: 'How many bats have been compelled to yield up their wickets just when they fancied they had made a fine draw, because the marvellous quickness of his eye, the wonderful activity of his movements, and the gifted use of either hand, have enabled Mr Jenner to clutch the ball.'

Jenner was an elegant and graceful man who stood further back from the wicket than Wenman, some 5 or 6 feet, and walked forward to meet the ball. His reactions were electric. At the lift of a heel, he would skim off the bails. Active, athletic, with a quick eye and unbounding energy, he relished the stumping chance above all else, but was eagerly about the pitch in search of work.

A delightful man and generous host, he followed his profession in the law almost to the exclusion of cricket after 1836, but he is reputed to have played in a match in 1880 at the age of seventy-four. He died in 1904 in his ninety-ninth year, having lived a very full life.

Two years before Jenner left the cricketing scene in 1836, Tom Box made his debut for the Players at Lord's, and there were many who considered him to be Jenner's equal as a wicket-keeper.

Box was a Sussex man, born at Ardingley, near Cuckfield, in 1809. He was short – 5 feet 7 inches – broad-faced, with side whiskers akin to those sported by Godfrey Evans since his retirement. He echoed Jenner in grace and elegance, although he could not rival the amateur in agility.

In every respect Box marked the transition from the pioneering years to the modern age of wicket-keeping. He had initially played for Sussex in 1828, the year that the bowler was first allowed to raise his hand to elbow level. The year after he first played for the Players, the bowler was permitted to raise his hand to shoulder level. The changes in the bowler's delivery effected a change in Box's style of wicket-keeping. He had begun in the upright style favoured by his predecessors and contemporaries; he ended with something close to a crouch that anticipated the stance of the late twentieth century, and had donned leg-guards and gauntlets. Sir Pelham Warner described him as 'one of the first of the great wicket-keepers'.

He was essentially a Sussex man, not missing a single county engagement for twenty-four seasons, but William Clarke enlisted him for his famous All England XI as the side's regular wicket-keeper.

He was for some years manager of the old Sussex ground in Ireland's Gardens. When that ground closed he moved to the Brunswick ground at Hove, which remained the Sussex headquarters until 1871 when the turf was removed to its present home. Box moved on to the Prince's ground in Cadogan Square, London, and it was there that he died quite suddenly while working the telegraph during the Middlesex and Nottinghamshire match of 1876. It was, perhaps, the ideal death for a man who had dedicated his life to the game.

Box improved as a batsman over the years, and, by some irony, in his last match for the Players, in 1853, he appears not to have kept wicket; unlike Wenman, Herbert Jenner-Fust and G. T. Knight, he had not been in the habit of keeping wicket at one end and bowling at the other. He was the first man really to have won his place in a first-class side solely on account of his wicket-keeping.

3

Blackham:
the 'Prince of Wicket-keepers'

Fourteen years before Tom Box died, an incident occurred in the match between England and Surrey at the Oval which was to alter the course of cricket and, for a time, to make the life of the wicket-keeper a very hard one.

Edgar Willsher of Kent was no-balled seven successive times by umpire John Lillywhite for raising his hand higher than his shoulder. The game was suspended for the day, and the following morning Lillywhite was replaced when he stubbornly refused to change his mind about the legality of Willsher's bowling. This incident, more than any other, led to the approval of overarm bowling, and in 1864 the wording of the law was changed so that the high-armed bowling action became legalized.

Unfortunately, the legalization of the high-armed bowling action did not coincide with an improvement in the standard of wickets, and wicket-keeping became a nightmarish and dangerous art, and particularly savage at Lord's, where sheep still grazed.

Box had been succeeded by some fine keepers, notably Tom Lockyer of Surrey, and now came a new generation, with men like Pinder and Pooley contending with fierce bowlers and uncertain wickets so that the long-stop remained a vital position on the field. Pinder of Yorkshire, like Plumb of Buckinghamshire, was one, however, who was prepared to stand up at the wicket to the fastest of bowling without the insurance of a long-stop.

It is impossible to say who was the first to have dispensed with a long-stop and stood up to fast bowling, but one of the first to gain a reputation for this deed and to earn himself the accolade among his colleagues of being called 'Prince of Wicket-keepers', was Richard Pilling of Lancashire.

A most popular man, Pilling was a wicket-keeper of the quiet and efficient school. He adopted a crouched attitude right on top of the stumps for all kinds of bowling, and his style was described as 'the perfection of neatness and rapidity'. He was born in Bedford in fact, but, having learned the art of the stone mason, he made his home in Accrington and played cricket for Lancashire. He over-shadowed his rivals – Lyttleton, Sherwin and Tylecote – and played eight times for England, for whom he caught ten and stumped four batsmen. But from the other side of the world came a man who was to win his title of 'Prince of Wicket-keepers' from him. 'Pilling,' wrote H. S. Altham, 'has possibly had no superior in the history of the game except Blackham.'

Throughout the history of the game there have always been rivals for the title of leading wicket-keeper – Ames or Duckworth? Knott or Taylor? Carter or Oldfield? – and, more than a century later, the arguments on the comparable merits of Blackham and Pilling will never be resolved. Sadly, Pilling was not to stay long in the contest. He had never been a man of robust health. On his first tour to Australia in 1882 he had suffered from sunstroke, although he recovered in time to play in the Test matches. He kept for Lancashire until the end of 1889, but during the winter he contracted influenza which developed into consumption, so he could not play in 1890. The Lanca-shire Club sent him to Australia to convalesce, but he died in March 1891, a few days after his return to England. He was thirty-five years old.

Pilling had always said that in no circumstances could he stand back, but there were times when Blackham stood back to Spofforth, although not many. The greatest praise that a man can earn is that given him by those who have played with and against him, and Lilley, the great England wicket-keeper, wrote of Blackham:

The first important match I had the pleasure of taking part in introduced me to the incomparable Blackham. I never had the opportunity of seeing Pilling, who I know was generally regarded as the prince of wicket-keepers of his time, and I am therefore unable to make any comparison; but I have no hesitation in saying that Mr J. M'C. Blackham was the greatest wicket-keeper I have ever had the privilege of seeing. His enthusiasm was boundless, his dexterity remarkable, and his fairness unquestionable.

It was a splendid education for me to watch the perfect movements of this great player. There was no straining after effect nor any suggestion of the acrobat, which is occasionally an unfortunate feature with some wicket-keepers. His judgement was so perfect in estimating the probable destination of a ball after delivery that, together with his method of placing himself for the readiest means of taking it, he could stop the most difficult delivery with the maximum of ease.

This is great praise indeed, and it hides the struggle that John McCarthy Blackham had in order to establish himself and become a national hero and an Australian legend.

He was born in Fitzroy, a suburb of Melbourne, on 11 May 1853. His early cricket was played with the Carlton Club and, like Oldfield, Ames and several others, he was not, initially, a wicket-keeper, being selected for his stubborn left-handed batting and his change bowling.

It is remarkable how often a chance practice match can change the course of a cricketer's career. Eifion Jones, that stalwart of the county championship, tells how he joined Glamorgan as a batsman and was at practice in the nets at Cardiff one day, when Phil Clift, the coach, asked him to put on the wicket-keeping gloves as David Evans was not available and they needed a keeper. Four days later, he kept wicket in a Club and Ground match at Maesteg, and that began a career which has lasted nearly a quarter of a century.

Something similar happened to Blackham. A cancelled fixture brought a scratch practice match and saw him behind the stumps for the first time. He was chosen as a wicket-keeper for the second XI and was discovered by

John Conway, who was to manage the first Australian XI. Conway persuaded him to join South Melbourne.

His reputation as a wicket-keeper grew, and in 1874 he played his first game for Victoria. It was the beginning of a first-class career that was to last for twenty years.

In March 1877 James Lillywhite's professional touring team, arriving hot from New Zealand where wicket-keeper Pooley had been detained after a fracas, played a combined Melbourne and Sydney XI at Melbourne cricket ground. The match was later to be labelled 'Australia *v.* England' and known as the first Test match.

Blackham kept wicket for Australia, but his inclusion caused dissent. *Scores and Biographies* states that 'Spofforth refused to assist because his own wicket-keeper, W. L. Murdoch, did not play'.

William Lloyd Murdoch was the first great Australian batsman and the first player to score a double century in a Test match, but he had begun as a wicket-keeper at Sydney University. In the face of Blackham's success behind the stumps, he concentrated solely on his batting, although occasionally, when on tour, he would keep wicket while Blackham fielded. On his last tour of England in 1890, however, he said that he found keeping wicket distasteful, although this did not prevent him from keeping wicket for England in the second innings of the Test match against South Africa at Cape Town in 1892.

Evidently, Spofforth was sufficiently impressed by Blackham's performance in the first Test match, for he played in the return match in Melbourne, when Murdoch also played, as a batsman, and Spofforth's first wicket in Test cricket was when Alfred Shaw was stumped by Blackham for 1.

Spofforth, it should be remembered, was to be named 'The Demon', as he frightened English batsmen into submission. W. G. Grace described him as 'terrifically fast', although other contemporary assessments reduced him to 'medium pace'. In truth, like Malcolm Marshall today, he varied his pace according to the wicket, but it must be recalled that in 1877 wickets had not reached the placidity and flatness that they were to attain in the subsequent twenty-five years, and Blackham's achievements in stumping batsmen off his bowling were remarkable by any standards.

He was twenty-three years old when the first Test match was played. He stood 5 feet 9½ inches tall, wore a black beard, and was protected only by the flimsiest of gloves and the thinnest of pads. He was a swarthy figure and stood with his feet splayed wider than is customary today. He placed himself exceptionally close to the wicket and was marvellously quick. He caught the ball and whipped off the bails in one motion, thereby thrilling spectators who had never seen the like before and bringing a new pressure on the batsman.

His success in those first two Tests was emphasized when compared with the performances of the two Englishmen, Selby and Jupp, who shared the job in Pooley's absence – 'neither proved equal to the job'.

George Giffen, the great Australian all-rounder who played with Blackham, had no doubts as to his wicket-keeper's greatness:

One could not help admiring him as he stood behind the stumps at critical periods of a game. With dark eyes as keen as a hawk, and regardless of knocks, he would take the fastest bowling with marvellous dexterity, and woe betide the batsman who even so much as lifted the heel of his back foot as he played forward and missed the ball.

Yet his position as wicket-keeper was still threatened by Murdoch when in 1878 he made the first of his eight tours to England. The match in which the Australians established their great reputation was their first at Lord's when, under D. W. Gregory's leadership, they beat a strong MCC side by 9 wickets in a day.

Nearly 5000 people saw Spofforth take 6 for 4 and 5 for 16 as W. G. Grace, Hornby, Alfred Shaw and the rest were bowled out for 33 and 19, while the Australians made 41 and 12 for 1 – and batsmen today complain about the wickets!

Blackham could find no place in that side and Murdoch

kept wicket, stumping Shaw and Vernon off Spofforth in the first innings.

Blackham returned for the victory over Yorkshire and played his first match at Lord's in the game with Middlesex which saw the Hon. E. Lyttleton score 113, but the Australians won by 98 runs. There was, of course, no Test match on this tour, but Blackham had captured the imagination of the English public just as he had captured the adulation of his own countrymen. The long-stop had disappeared, for Blackham is reputed to have asked one of his captains why a man had been placed behind him and told the skipper, 'Put him out where he can do some good.'

This disappearance of the long-stop did not please all, and there is a legend that a group of English clergymen complained that, in bringing about the abolition of the long-stop, Blackham had endangered the well-being of cricket by being responsible for taking away the clergy's traditional fielding spot in village teams.

One of his most notable achievements in that first tour of 1878, a tour that began in Brisbane in November 1877 and closed at Inglewood in January 1879, was in a match against Eighteen of Stockport at Stockport. On a rough, crude and bumpy wicket he caught four and stumped six batsmen, and people marvelled at his skill.

He played in the Test match of 1879 at Melbourne and, a month later, on the same ground, he stumped five English batsmen in the first innings when Victoria beat Lord Harris's English XI.

In 1880 he was in England again and had by now reached the pinnacle, indisputably the greatest wicket-keeper that the game had ever known. Harry Altham wrote in his *History of Cricket*: 'Once more did Blackham's wicket-keeping astonish all who saw it, and the way that day after day on all sorts of wickets he stood up to all his bowlers was a revelation to English cricket.'

On 6, 7 and 8 September the first Test match in England was played at Kennington Oval. The attendances on the first two days were the highest that had ever been known at a cricket match at that time. W. G. Grace scored England's first-ever Test century; Murdoch, who was the Australian captain, hit 153 not out when Australia followed-on; but England won by 5 wickets. *Wisden* remarked that 'the fielding and wicket-keeping on both sides was splendid', and all reports consistently claimed that the wicket-keeping of Blackham and the Hon. Alfred Lyttleton was the finest exhibition of the art that had yet been seen.

Blackham was to play in every one of the first seventeen Test matches – a unique record. Once, at Sydney in 1882, Murdoch kept wicket for most of the match, and at Lord's in 1886 Jarvis was the wicket-keeper; but from that first Test in 1877, until his thirty-fifth and last in 1894, Blackham remained the supreme wicket-keeper in the world.

He became captain of Victoria in 1882–3 and led the side for five seasons, while he first captained Australia at Sydney in March 1885. He led them on his eighth and last tour of England in 1893. He was not noted, however, as being a good captain, and there have in fact been very few successful wicket-keeper-captains in the history of the game.

Blackham had a tendency to worry over temporary setbacks. It is strange that a man who was so quiet and calm as a wicket-keeper should be such a fidget and a worrier as a captain; but a worrier he was, losing a stone on the 1893 tour of England, and pacing up and down the pavilion like a caged lion when things were not going well. Certainly, he was a first-class analyser of the opposition and was very quick to detect a batsman's weaknesses, but his temperament was highly strung and in a tense situation off the field he would retreat into the agony of his own nerves.

His last Test match was a historic one. It saw A. C. MacLaren and Joe Darling make their international debuts, and Blackham, as Australia's captain, endure the cruellest twists of fate.

On 14 December 1894 in the burning heat he won the toss, and by the end of the day George Giffen had scored 161 and Syd Gregory was unbeaten on 85. Next day

Blackham joined Gregory when the score was 409 for 8. They added 154, which remains a record, and Gregory made 201, the first Test double century in Australia. Blackham and Jones added 23 for the last wicket before Blackham was bowled by Richardson. He had made 74, his highest score in Test cricket. Australia, who had been 21 for 3, totalled 586.

Giffen took 4 wickets and Turner 2 as Australia nibbled away at the England batting and dismissed them for 325. Blackham caught Brockwell off Jones and stumped Ford off Giffen, but towards the end of the innings he gave 2 overs – six-ball overs in Australia in 1894 – to the fast-medium Lyons. Lyons bowled 2 maiden overs and with one delivery he split Blackham's thumb, during the eighth-wicket stand between Briggs and Lockwood. The injury marked the end of Blackham's career.

England followed-on and scored 437 in their second innings. Australia needed 177 to win, and by the close of the fifth day, they were 113 for 2. Harry Altham relates what happened:

George Giffen has told us that when he woke on the next morning and found the sun streaming in at his window he was in ecstasy, but that the first man he met was Blackham, 'with a face as long as a coffee-pot'. It had poured half the night, the wicket was as sticky as it could be, and once again, as before and thereafter, we had left-hand bowling to use it decisively. Peel and Briggs were unplayable, and England won by 10 runs!

Blackham went in at number eleven and was caught and bowled by Peel for 2.

So ended the career of the 'Prince of Wicket-keepers'. He remained superbly fit, his weight in his early years never being above 10 stone 6 pounds. As to the state of his hands, after twenty years of keeping in what were little more than gardening gloves, there are varying reports. Lord Harris stated that they were free from swellings, but Lord Hawke, for whom Blackham was 'the greatest of wicket-keepers', wrote: 'As for Blackham at the wicket, well, he conjured. His hands were all gnarled and his fingers misshapen from blows, but he never winced. Quick as the proverbial lightning, he could take any bowling apparently as if it were aimed to come straight to his hands, and he was the W. G. of his own department.'

For the Australians, he had become a folk hero. Black-bearded, neat, the essence of reliability, he worked as a clerk in the Colonial Bank in Melbourne. Before the end of his career he had been dubbed 'Old Jack' by the crowd. It was a term of affection that he shared with the great racehorse, Carbine.

Blackham lived until he was nearly eighty, dying three days after Christmas, 1932. He had set standards which, for a hundred years, others have striven to emulate.

4

'Dick' Lilley:
a Model of Consistency

Just before the fourth Test match on 2, 3, 5 and 6 February 1912, MCC played Victoria in Melbourne in a match for the benefit of John McCarthy Blackham. It was overpoweringly hot, 106°F in the shade on the first day, and the intense heat restricted the attendance. The gross receipts for the match were £290, whereas £1183 had been taken when MCC and Victoria had met earlier in the tour. As MCC took £122 from the match, the amount left for Blackham must have been small, but four years earlier £1359 had been raised for him, a testimony to the affection in which he was held by the Australian public.

It is interesting to note, however, that two years before Blackham's benefit, a match had been played in Sydney between New South Wales and Australia for the benefit of James Joseph Kelly, and £1400 had been collected. Kelly, thirteen years younger than Blackham, was the great man's successor in the Australian team and had just decided to retire from Test cricket when his benefit was arranged. He had toured England in 1905 but a damaged finger and a blow over the heart by a ball from Walter Brearley prompted him to retire at the end of that tour.

Like Blackham, he stood up to most bowlers and was renowned for having taken eight catches in the fourth Test at Sydney in 1902. He also gained credit as a batsman, being top scorer with 8 when MCC bowled out the Australians for 18 at Lord's in 1896, his first appearance there, and shared an unbeaten eighth-wicket stand of 25 in an hour with Hugh Trumble to give Australia

victory by 3 wickets in the historic second Test at Old
Trafford in the same year.

Kelly was born in Port Melbourne and moved to
Sydney and New South Wales when it became apparent
to him that he would not displace the mighty Blackham
in the Victoria side. He is credited with 355 dismissals in
his career, but there is debate as to whether 112 or 113
of them were stumpings. Blackham is credited with 272
catches and 179 stumpings. In Test matches Kelly had
63 dismissals and Blackham 60, having played one game
less; but none would ever suggest that Kelly was on a par
with Blackham, for although statistics give some indica-
tion, it is not by figures alone that a wicket-keeper's worth
can be assessed.

Over fifty years ago Norman J. Pogson advocated a
table to show wicket-keeping prowess alongside the
batting and bowling averages. He had made a statistical
survey of international wicket-keepers and wished to draw
up comparisons on the following lines:

Possibilities: Credit the wicket-keeper. Every ball bowled is of
vital interest to the wicket-keeper. He has to move to receive it
in case it misses the batsman by a fraction. The total of balls
bowled in a match gives an idea of the work a wicket-keeper
has had to prepare for. Byes should be reckoned not so much
on the runs scored as on the balls bowled.

Actualities: Credit the wicket-keeper with the wickets taken by
him. Allow also for a proportion of those 'run out'. Do not
forget that the score sheet never shows how many chances the
wicket-keeper has offered to him. Because he does not catch or
stump a man is no sign of poor form.

Mistakes: Byes alone can be laid to a wicket-keeper. Leg-byes
may have gone any way. Credit the wicket-keeper with the facts
that: (a) the bowling may have been frightfully erratic; (b) the
bowling may have been beating the bat, the wicket and the
wicket-keeper; (c) four byes may have come off one, and even
the last ball of an otherwise faultless innings.

Mr Pogson asserted that this method should be a sound
one by which to judge, but one must treat it with much
scepticism. It is full of ambiguities and half-truths. How

can one credit the wicket-keeper with the fact that the bowling 'may have been frightfully erratic'?

The ultimate assessment of a wicket-keeper, as of any fielder, is an impressionistic one. Joanna Lewis, daughter of the writer, broadcaster and former England Test captain, Tony Lewis, carried out an interesting survey during the England tour of Australia in 1982-3. With the England side in the field, she marked down every time a man fielded the ball. At the end of the day her figures were revealing. The two players who had touched the ball least were Gower and Randall, by common consent the two best fielders on the England side.

There is no statistical evaluation possible in order to assess the worth of a wicket-keeper. In the end, it is self-evaluation that matters.

Paul Downton, a highly intelligent young man who thinks deeply about the game, says that each day he strives for perfection. He goes on to the field determined that he will take everything cleanly, not just the balls that are bowled to him, but also the returns from the deep field. He remembers having achieved his ambition once – in Antigua when he was with the England party in the West Indies in 1981. 'I didn't drop a ball all day,' he recalls, 'whether from a return or from taking the bowlers. I felt at least I had achieved it once.'

Arthur Frederick Augustus Lilley would have agreed with Paul Downton. He wrote:

Wicket-keeping, like so many other things, is only too frequently judged more by results than by merit. I have on many an occasion kept wicket in a manner that has been quite satisfactory to myself, and, not to be too modest, have been quite pleased with my day's work. But, unaccompanied as it has been with the dismissal of any of my opponents, it has quite failed to attract attention. But there can have been no opportunities if the batsmen have offered no chance; the bowling has not beaten the bat sufficiently. But when the bowling has been of a character to provide chances which the wicket-keeper has been able to accept, his work is more generally appreciated, though not necessarily better.

'Dick' Lilley kept wicket for England thirty-five times between 1896 and 1909, by which time he was forty-three years old. Few players of his time, save MacLaren and Hayward, approached his number of Tests for England. In these, he caught 70 and stumped 22 batsmen. He was also called upon to bowl his leg-breaks from time to time, and in the Manchester Test of 1896 he took the wicket of the Australian skipper G. H. S. Trott, so breaking a stubborn stand.

On leaving school in Birmingham, where he was born, Lilley had gone to work for Cadbury Brothers at Bournville, and it was here that he first had the chance to play club cricket. The Bournville Cricket and Football Club only came into existence just after Lilley had begun to work for the firm, and he first won his place in the side as a bowler. Like so many other great wicket-keepers, Lilley came to the job by accident.

George Cadbury, one of those great Liberal social reformers of the nineteenth century, encouraged the new sports club by hiring a coach for them, and Shilton, the jovial Warwickshire professional who loved three things in life – batting, bowling and talking – came along some evenings to give advice to the cricket team.

One evening the club's regular wicket-keeper was absent and Shilton asked for a volunteer to go behind the stumps. Lilley came forward and Shilton gave him some basic advice on how to stand and how to take the ball. Lilley felt completely at home in his new position and made a good enough impression to keep wicket for Bournville for the rest of the season.

At the beginning of the following season, 1888, he was invited to play for Warwickshire Club and Ground in a match at Smethwick. A month later, on 11 and 12 May, he made his first-class debut when he kept wicket for Warwickshire against the Australian touring side. He was to keep his place in the county side for the next twenty-three years.

Quite tall, with more of an upright stance than most keepers, he was sound, calm and neat in all he did. There was no fuss with 'Dick' Lilley. He was so consistent an artist that at the end of his career his hands and fingers showed scarcely a trace of the heavy strain to which they must have been subjected over the years in keeping wicket to such a variety of bowling. There were other, more flamboyant wicket-keepers, but there was no safer catcher of the ball.

Wisden was rather grudging in its praise of Lilley, stating that 'there have been greater wicket-keepers to fast bowling', although admitting that he was a 'marvel of consistency'.

The comment regarding Lilley's keeping to fast bowling is a reflection on his tendency to stand back and to be one of the first to do so consistently. He began his career by standing up close to the wicket to all bowlers, but it was W. G. Grace who changed his philosophy:

One of my earliest experiences in keeping wicket to Richardson was at the time when I usually stood close up to all fast bowlers, and so on this occasion, too, I thought it was quite correct to stand up to Richardson. But Dr W. G. Grace, who was captain of the team, thought differently, and at once suggested I should do better by standing back. I, of course, accepted the doctor's advice, and undoubtedly it was the wiser policy to pursue, as I succeeded in catching out three batsmen. By standing back one is able to cover so much more ground for the purpose of making catches, and, as at the same time one has very few opportunities of stumping off fast bowling, I am sure it is the right thing to do, and so ever afterwards I invariably adopted this policy.

This was the beginning of the great debate on whether a wicket-keeper should stand up or back to pace bowling, but it must be remembered that it was a question of standing back to bowlers like Tom Richardson who was quick, and not to the medium-pace trundlers of today.

Lilley first played for England against Australia at Lord's in 1896, and he kept his place in the side for the other two Tests of the series; but he was unable to accept an invitation from A. E. Stoddart to tour Australia in 1897–8 and Bill Storer of Derbyshire kept in that series.

Storer stood up to the fastest bowling, even to Charles

Kortright. He was an upright, elegant and delicate wicket-keeper and a good batsman. He kept his place in the England side for the first Test match against Australia at Trent Bridge in 1899.

Storer had some difficult bowling to take at Derbyshire and Lilley was full of praise for him:

Hulme in particular was a most difficult bowler to take, and he was left-handed, and could make the ball either come with his arm or swing from the off. As all wicket-keepers know, this is the most difficult bowling of all to handle, and I do not think it possible for anyone to have taken it better than Storer did.

This is interesting to read, for it shows a change in fashion: the majority of wicket-keepers today would say that it is the off-break bowler who poses the greatest problems.

Lilley had the highest regard for Storer:

I consider Storer was one of the very finest wicket-keepers of his time, and probably only equalled by Mr Gregor MacGregor. Standing up to fast bowling I do not think there can have been the slightest question that they were then the two best in England. They both possessed a delightfully easy style, either on the off- or the leg-side, and their efforts were always a great treat to watch. I have seen them many times do some particularly fine work, and have keenly appreciated its brilliancy.

Storer's wicket-keeping was remarkable for the quickness he showed when moving to a ball on the leg-side. In doing so he did not move from his original position, but was always able to gather the ball with ease, and thus create for himself the maximum of certainty in taking a possible catch or effecting a possible stumping – one of those things, I think, which well illustrates the perfection of wicket-keeping.

However much Storer was esteemed by Lilley, the first Test match at Trent Bridge in 1899 was his sixth and last for England. Lilley returned for the second Test and remained England's first-choice wicket-keeper for the next decade.

He stuck to the principle learned from W. G. Grace, that it was invariably better to stand back to the fast bowlers. He recalled that the best catch he ever made was in the first innings of the fifth Test of 1902 when, standing back to the bowling of George Hirst, he caught R. A. Duff by making about 2 yards on the leg-side and holding a shot that would have gone to the boundary.

His dignified bearing gave Lilley an air of authority, and this was enhanced, not just by the military moustache, but by his astute judgement of the game. Captains at county and Test level recognized his qualities of perception and knowledge of opponents, and frequently consulted him. In his own right, he was a respected captain of the Players.

He kept himself superbly fit and played soccer in the winter to supplement his summer income. He was warned against playing because of the injury risk involved, but his reply was as positive as everything he did: 'I can assure you I don't play because I like the game. I play because it helps me to get a living in the winter, for what I can get by playing cricket would not keep me in the winter as well.' Nothing changes very much.

He made his first trip to Australia in 1901–2 and his second and last in 1903–4. It was on the latter trip that he first kept wicket to Bosanquet. He had not seen Bosanquet bowl before the team arrived in Australia, nor had he had any experience of googly bowling. He positioned himself behind the net at the ground in Adelaide where Bosanquet first practised, and studied the googly bowler's action. He was impressed by the way in which Bosanquet could completely hide the type of ball that he was going to bowl, and he decided that it was impossible to anticipate which way the ball would break.

He kept wicket to Bosanquet for the first time in the opening match of the tour, against South Australia in Adelaide. His assessment of the situation is interesting, reflecting as it does what must have been Lilley's reliance on his own powers of concentration:

. . . after I had taken the first few overs I began to understand him, and so felt more confidence in taking him. There was no understanding existing between us, which I think is much better for the bowler, so far as this particular kind of bowling is concerned. He has nothing else to think about other than beating the batsman, and if he should also occasionally succeed in beating the wicket-keeper, it is preferable to allowing his bowling to suffer in the slightest.

Bosanquet's great success on the tour came in the fourth Test at Sydney where Australia, chasing 329 to win, were bowled out for 171, Bosanquet taking 6 for 51, including a spell of 5 for 12. Lilley thought that Bosanquet's bowling was good enough to get out any side on any wicket and that such bowling was helpful to a wicket-keeper in providing him with opportunities to dismiss batsmen. In that particular innings, Lilley took a catch and made three stumpings. In the seven Test matches that Bosanquet played, Lilley was always the wicket-keeper and he assisted Bosanquet with a catch and eight stumpings out of his 25 wickets.

He did not believe, however, that a record number of dismissals reflected a wicket-keeper's expertise. In the Whitsun holiday match against Worcestershire in 1906 he took four catches and made two stumpings in the first innings. *Wisden* made no comment on the feat, although it was then a record, and six dismissals was a performance Lilley accomplished three times in his career. He was, however, sanguine about such records:

I know on plenty of occasions when I have kept wicket quite well enough to satisfy myself it has brought no success with it, whereas on other occasions I have had most success when least satisfied. Strictly speaking, a wicket-keeper must not be judged merely by what he does, but also by what he fails to do; not by the chances he accepts, or the lack of opportunity, but by the opportunities he misses.

He knew well that there were days when crucial chances were missed, for he had been involved in two bizarre incidents that had cost England two Test matches. In the second Test match of 1896, the game in which Ranjitsinhji had made his Test debut and in which Kelly and Trumble had steered Australia to a narrow victory, Lilley had dropped Kelly when Australia were still 9 runs short of their target. He had taken the snick cleanly enough, but as he pulled his arm back, he struck his thigh and knocked the ball out of his hands.

On the same ground, Old Trafford, six years later in the famous match which saw Fred Tate drop a vital catch in his one and only Test, Lilley was batting with Wilfred Rhodes with 8 runs needed for victory and 2 wickets standing. He hit Trumble for a fierce and fine shot to leg for what looked to be a certain 4, but the ball was held back a little by the wind, and Clem Hill, running at top speed round the boundary for more than 30 yards, took a marvellous one-handed catch which has become a legend in the history of Test match cricket. Then there was rain, and on the resumption of the match Fred Tate was out and Australia won by 3 runs.

Lilley's final appearance for England was at the Oval in the last Test match of the 1909 series against Australia. It was in this match that D. W. Carr made his only international appearance and Frank Woolley made his Test debut. Lilley stumped Victor Trumper off Carr in the second innings of the drawn match, and then he was gone from the Test scene, replaced by Herbert Strudwick and his colleague from Warwickshire, 'Tiger' Smith.

Earlier in the year Lilley had represented the Players for the last time when he captained them to victory at the Oval, and at the end of the season he virtually retired from wicket-keeping, although he continued to play for Warwickshire for another two seasons as a batsman.

E. J. 'Tiger' Smith was already displaying fine form when given the opportunity, and Lilley was now into his forties. Frank Foster, fast-medium left-arm, had come into the Warwickshire side in 1908 at the age of nineteen, and within three years he was to captain them to their first County Championship. It was the arrival of Foster that marked the end of Lilley's career. Good as his hands were, apart from a dislocated joint on his trigger finger, which necessitated a light-pull trigger on the gun with which he won the gold stick at Monte Carlo, they had nevertheless taken a hammering over the years and Foster was a difficult man for him to take. He engendered considerable pace from the wicket off a deceptively lazy run-up, and there was a lot to take on the leg-side. He kept splitting the webbing of Lilley's fingers.

'Tiger' Smith felt that Lilley was as much a victim of poor equipment as of advancing years: 'The gloves we had to wear in those days were very thin. They were made of felt, there was no padding; they were more like mittens so you had to take the ball correctly.' Yet for twenty-three years Lilley had kept wicket with this scant protection, and Smith had no doubts as to his quality: 'He was so unfussy and solid and in all the time I watched him, I never saw him on his backside; he knew just how far he could reach behind the stumps.'

Lilley gave only two pieces of advice: forget about dropped catches and get to the returns from the field in order to save overthrows.

At one time he kept a public house and also partnered Billy Quaife in a sports business, but he was essentially a loner and eventually, following a dispute, Quaife bought him out.

His end with Warwickshire was a sad one. He was undoubtedly one of the most knowledgeable of cricketers, and as a senior player of vast experience, he had been used to giving advice to England captains. So it was no surprise that he should take it upon himself to instruct Foster, a man half his age, as to what to do when Warwickshire were poised to win their first County Championship.

Foster did not resent advice, but he was determined to be captain and to keep matters in his own hands. The affair came to a head in the match against Yorkshire at Harrogate at the end of July 1911. When David Denton came out to bat, Lilley, without consulting the skipper, waved several fielders into deeper positions. Denton played a lofted cover drive and Lilley anticipated the shot. He gave his orders loud enough for the spectators to hear them, and Foster, to his credit, told the older man to mind his own business; he would accept advice if Lilley came to him, but he did not intend to be made to look a

41

fool. As he wrote later, 'It was essential that I, as captain, had no rival or opposition.'

When Foster went to the players' dressing room to lead them on to the field after lunch, there was dead silence, and he realized that if they were to win the championship, they must avoid internal disharmony at all costs.

Warwickshire won the game at Harrogate and then drew at Southampton. When Foster was asked by the committee about the team for the next match, his advice was simple: 'Drop Dick.' Lilley resigned from the club and Foster had no further interruption from any member of the Warwickshire team as he led them to the title.

'Tiger' Smith says that the way in which Lilley was treated by the committee and the fact that he was left out of the official championship team photograph soured the feelings of the players; but Lilley attended the victory dinner at the Grand Hotel at the end of September, where he was one of the speakers and where he received a special retirement presentation.

He then moved down to Bristol and, after the First World War, was a member of the special advisory committee which helped to re-establish the Gloucester-shire County Cricket Club. He died on 17 November 1929, within a day of completing his sixty-second year.

He had had an honourable career, quiet and superbly efficient. Perhaps the lack of fuss distracted the unknowing from a true appreciation of his worth. Sir Pelham Warner wrote of him in the *Westminster Gazette*, when he retired from the game in August 1911:

He has had a long innings and a glorious career. . . . As a wicket-keeper he was very good indeed, safe, sure, and quick, and with a model style. There are many good judges who are of the opinion that he was never, at any time during his career, the absolutely best wicket-keeper in England; but one can only speak from one's own experience, and my idea is that I never saw a more reliable stumper.

5

'Tiger' Smith:
a Much-loved Man

Before Lilley's distinguished career had come to an end, his successor, Ernest James 'Tiger' Smith, was already in the side.

Lilley had played against, admired and learned from Blackham. Smith revered and learned from Lilley, and so the line continued. Smith and Lilley had much in common.

'Tiger' Smith was born in 1886 near the centre of the city of Birmingham in Benacre Street, a street which has since vanished in the maze of fly-overs, underpasses and ring roads which constitute the city centre. He lived a mile from Edgbaston and he adored cricket, although the only games he played as a boy were scratch games in the park and in the street. His parents had died by the time he was thirteen and his was the struggle for survival in the late nineteenth century.

He had first watched cricket when he was ten, clinging to a tree outside the Edgbaston ground, when Warwickshire played Kent. Three years later he was at work. Like Lilley, he joined Bournville, earning 5s. 10d. a week for fifty-eight hours' work.

It was at Bournville that he lost the top joints of the third and little fingers of his right hand and of the little finger of his left hand. He worked in the factory and they were 'chewed off' by a machine when he was fourteen years old.

A year after this accident he went to watch his brother Harold play for Bournville's third team. The regular wicket-keeper was ill and had not arrived for the match, so young Smith was told that he was to keep wicket; he was given the pads and gloves and told to get on with it. He was a natural and found the job presented him with no difficulties whatsoever. Quickly he climbed to the second team, but he was reluctant to move into the first XI, where the players were older and 'too flighty and full of airs'.

The professional coach at Bournville at the time was Albert Bird, who played for Worcestershire, and he recommended Smith to his county. The lad from the back streets of Birmingham was seventeen when he went for a month's trial to Worcestershire. They were obviously impressed, for they asked Warwickshire's permission to register the young man. Warwickshire refused permission and invited Smith to play for them, his native county. He began his association with them in 1904. It was a stormy friendship that was to last for seventy-five years.

He played his first game for Warwickshire against the South African touring side of 1904, and he remembered that his first dropped catch was when he put down Louis Tancred off Sam Hargreave when the batsman was on 7. He went on to make 106. He was ever grateful to Hargreave for shouting down the wicket at him, 'Never mind, young 'un, you'll miss a few more before you're finished.' Smith used to say later that he never missed a catch, but a few did drop out.

For a time he was seconded to the MCC and he played with and against W. G. Grace for his London County XI although he did not play first-class cricket for the great man's team. His memory of Grace was that if the old man thought you were no good, he would go out and buy a rabbit and put it in your cricket bag.

By 1910, with Lilley having given up wicket-keeping, Smith was established in the Warwickshire side, and he acquitted himself well. The following year Warwickshire won the County Championship for the first time.

This was the significant year for Smith. Halfway through the season Warwickshire were close to the bottom of the table, but they won thirteen matches out of twenty and carried off the championship. They were inspired by skipper Frank Foster, the twenty-two-year-old left-arm fast-medium bowler and forcing batsman, who scored 1383 runs and took 116 wickets, but Smith's contribution, too, was a fine one – 807 runs and 45 dismissals in the championship alone.

As already indicated, Foster's bowling heralded the end of Lilley's career behind the stumps, but it was also the making of 'Tiger' Smith. Foster bowled off a short run with an easy action and was said to possess that mythical increase of pace off the pitch which the scientists deny and which the batsman is certain exists. Occasionally the ball would straighten, but usually it went with his arm and the batsman found himself hurried into his shot. Generally, Foster placed six men on the leg-side for the right-hander, and he was consulted by Jardine before the 'bodyline' tour of 1932–3, although it must be added that he himself disapproved of Jardine's later tactics.

It was said that Foster gave as much trouble to his own wicket-keepers as he did to opposing batsmen with his swing and deceptive pace. It was generally accepted that the only wicket-keeper who could take him well was 'Tiger' Smith, who was big, robust, tall for a wicket-keeper and wonderfully agile. Of course, Smith stood up close to Foster and a quarter of his victims in the championship year were off the fast-medium left-armer.

Smith was chosen to represent the Players against the Gentlemen at Lord's in 1911. It was a historic match. Sir Pelham Warner described the teams as 'probably as good as ever played in this match'. It was Tom Hayward's last appearance in the fixture, and the Gentlemen won by 130 runs. J. W. H. T. Douglas and Foster had splendid matches and were selected to go to Australia the following winter with Warner's side, and Smith kept well to Sidney Barnes and was asked to go as understudy to Strudwick. There were some who considered him lucky to have been chosen ahead of Huish, Dolphin and others, but most felt that it was the correct choice. He had had a magnificent year.

It was during this tour that Warner fell ill after the first match and Johnny Douglas took over the captaincy.

Strudwick, as expected, played in the first Test match, which was lost. This was the game in which Douglas had caused concern by opening the bowling himself instead of Barnes. Smith maintained that Douglas would probably have opened in the second Test, too, had he not thrown the ball to Barnes at the end of Foster's first over instead of to the skipper.

Smith was a great admirer of Douglas, whom he considered to be straight. It was Douglas who decided that Smith would play in the second Test, Strudwick having had his chance in the first.

Strudwick was the model of courtesy and a great sportsman, but the two keepers had different attitudes towards practice. Warner was impressed because Strudwick kept in the nets, something which Smith declined to do. Smith kept a lacrosse ball in his pocket and would throw it against a wall for ten minutes every morning and try to take it. He maintained that it was quicker than an ordinary cricket ball and came off the wall sharply, and he was adamant that it helped his reactions throughout his career.

When dictating his memorable autobiography to Patrick Murphy, who so faithfully set it down, Smith said:

Struddy thought it was okay to practise in the orthodox manner behind the stumps in the nets, but I didn't agree. You're restricted in your movements in the nets, particularly on the leg-side. Another practising technique I used on that tour: I'd get a stump in the ground and ask Jack Hobbs, Jimmy Iremonger, Joe Vine and Sep Kinneir to throw at me from different angles in a wide circle. That way I adjusted to the extra bounce of Australian wickets and kept myself sharp by running around to take returns.

Foster was in no doubt that Smith's presence behind the stumps gave him an added advantage as a bowler. Smith was able to read Foster's signals, one of which – a change in step during the run up – indicated a slower delivery. They worked out a plan to restrict the three powerful Australian left-handers, Ransford, Bardsley and Clem Hill. It was decided that Foster should bowl at them outside the leg-stump, trying to induce overbalance and giving the opportunity for a leg-side stumping. The plan left little margin for error, but it had one dramatic result when Smith stumped Clem Hill first ball in the first innings of the third Test match at Adelaide. Warner considered it to be 'one of the technical masterpieces of the game'.

Foster had been bowling quickly and Smith had been standing back to him. He had already caught Bardsley standing up to Barnes, and when Hill came in, at 88 for 5, the Australian skipper having dropped down the order because of a slight indisposition, Smith moved up to take Foster.

Warner described what happened: '. . . by a prearranged plan the bowler sent down a ball on the leg-side; Hill shaped to glance it to leg, missed it, went out of his ground, and Smith put the wicket down.' It was a magnificent piece of work and Smith's keeping won high eulogy from all the critics.

He maintained that he also stumped Hill in the second innings when the Australian skipper was out by 'about twelve inches', but the umpire thought otherwise and Hill went on to make 98, which still did not prevent England winning by 7 wickets.

England had won the second Test match, Smith's debut, by 8 wickets, and went on to take the series 4–1. Smith's first catch in Test cricket had been during Barnes's famous opening spell of 4 for 3 at Melbourne. Barnes had bowled a quicker ball on the off-side and Warwick Armstrong had tried to cut, only to see Smith take the ball high by his right shoulder. Smith took two more catches that innings and, in the second innings, dismissed Ransford off Foster with 'a great catch on the leg-side'.

The general judgement was that Smith kept wicket very finely, being extraordinarily good on the leg-side. He played in all six Test matches for England during the miserable, rain-ruined Triangular Tournament of 1912, and England won four of them, two being washed out by rain.

It was not until Smith returned from Australia in 1912 that Warwickshire discovered that he had lost the tops of three fingers. He was congratulated on his performance by Howard Vaughton, the vice-chairman of the club, who noticed the missing joints. He was horrified and asked if the joints had been lost in Australia. Smith told him of the factory accident at Bournville when he was fourteen. Vaughton commented: 'If we had known about that, we wouldn't have taken you on the staff.'

One would have expected that Smith was now established as England's wicket-keeper for many years to come, but the ways of selectors have ever been strange, and these were the days of amateur dominance. In 1913 Smith had scored 971 runs and had 68 dismissals, the best haul of his career, but he was not chosen to tour South Africa that winter. He maintained that it was the custom for the amateurs to go to South Africa to enjoy the sunshine, and so it was D. C. Robinson of Gloucestershire who was asked to go as reserve wicket-keeper to Herbert Strudwick. However, Robinson's health gave way as soon as he reached South Africa and he returned home without playing in a single match. Smith had been kept on stand-by and at the end of October he was told to sail to South Africa.

There was a feeling that Smith would again squeeze Strudwick out of the side, for he was certainly the favourite of Douglas, the skipper, but, having arrived late, he played a relaxed part in the tour. He participated in only nine matches and kept wicket in only five of those.

He did play in the second Test match, however, as a batsman. He batted at number nine and scored 9. Barnes took 17 wickets and England won by an innings. Smith fielded at mid-on and caught Gerry Hartigan off the bowling of Wilfred Rhodes in the first innings. It was Rhodes's 110th Test wicket. Smith asserted that it was a dolly catch, that he would not have caught it otherwise for he did not like fielding. He disliked the ball being hit at him, and this was only the second first-class match in which he had not kept wicket.

It was his eleventh and last Test match. England had

won the nine Tests in which he had played and the other two had been ruined by the weather. There are very few other players who can boast such a Test career.

He joined the army when war broke out, but he was invalided out with cartilage trouble after an accident on the parade ground. He then worked with St John's Ambulance Brigade where he was to gain a knowledge of bone and muscle structure that he was to use to great advantage in later life.

When cricket resumed in 1919 he was thirty-three years old and he played for Warwickshire with consistent success for another eleven years, although, by his own admission, with never quite the same joy as he had had before the war.

He developed into a sound and attacking opening batsman, reaching 1000 runs a season six times after the war and scoring twenty centuries in all for Warwickshire. His highest score was 177 against Derbyshire in 1927, but the innings that gave him the most pleasure was when he scored 139 not out against Sussex at Edgbaston at the end of July 1925.

Warwickshire were set 391 to win, in just under 5 hours. Smith and Parsons put on 176 for the first wicket, and Smith and Calthorpe an unbeaten 216 for the second wicket, to win the match with 45 minutes to spare.

Smith played a significant part in the bizarre match between Warwickshire and Hampshire at Edgbaston in June 1922, in which Hampshire were bowled out for 15 in their first innings and then won by 155 runs. Tennyson was missed and the ball went through the fielder's hands for 4. Smith was unsighted to a leg-side ball from Howell which went for 4 byes. Four byes constituted more than a quarter of the total score and Warwickshire maintained that Hampshire should have been out for 7.

Although he played for the Players on several occasions in the 1920s, Smith did not play for England after 1913. *The Cricketer* advocated that he should have replaced Strudwick in the England side in 1921, but although over thirty players appeared for England in that dreadful year, Smith was not one of them.

When the Australians came to England in 1926 he was forty years old, but he was in magnificent form. In the match against Derbyshire at Edgbaston, he caught four and stumped three batsmen to equal the wicket-keeping record of seven dismissals in an innings.

At lunchtime during the match between Warwickshire and Nottinghamshire at Trent Bridge, Arthur Carr, the Notts captain and also captain of England, told Smith that he was to keep wicket for the North of England against the Australians.

The match was played at Edgbaston at the beginning of June, and Fred Root, bowling leg-theory, took 7 for 42 in the first innings. Smith had kept to Root on an MCC tour of the West Indies the previous winter and had always been very strong on the leg-side since he first kept to Frank Foster. He also kept well to Larwood, 'the quickest I've ever kept to', and Geary.

Warner asked Smith to come to Lord's for the Test trial which followed the match at Edgbaston. He was in the England side while Strudwick kept for the Rest:

I kept as well as at any time in my life against Tate, Gubby Allen, Macaulay, Kilner and Woolley. Arthur Gilligan said to me, 'Is that the first time you've kept to Maurice, Tiger?' I said, 'Yes, why?' and his reply was, 'Because you make it look so easy.' I was very pleased with my display and Warner told me I'd be in the Test team. It was announced the next day and Struddy was in.

He believed that that was really the end of him as a player, although it taught him much. He found it hard to understand, too, why George Brown was chosen after Strudwick had had a bad game at Lord's. Brown was little more than a makeshift keeper, although a good batsman and useful bowler.

Smith was considered gruff and unapproachable by some towards the end of his career, but those who knew him realized his wisdom and the warmth of his compassion. He often found himself in isolation in his position as senior professional, and there were disagreements with the committee.

In 1930 he scored over 1000 runs, hit three centuries and, according to *Wisden* kept wicket with 'considerable ability', but he was offered no new contract for 1931, only a request to play on a match fee basis. He declined and became a first-class umpire. In this area, too, he reached Test standard.

Smith was the first wicket-keeper to tape his fingers so that they wouldn't break, and he claimed that only once in his career did he suffer a finger injury. That was when he attempted to catch Gilbert Jessop down the leg-side off Frank Foster, and broke the second finger of his left hand. He played in the next match with a pad stuck between his first and second fingers.

He was given his nickname 'Tiger' by 'Dick' Lilley. The second-team youngsters had been playing cards to pass the time when rain had stopped play, and one of the bigger lads accused one of the smaller ones of cheating. A fight started and Smith laid out the big fellow. When the first team heard about it 'Dick' Lilley said. 'We'll call him "Tiger" Smith', which was the name of a noted boxer of the time.

As well as umpiring in his later years, he also coached youngsters in South Africa, and in 1946, having spent the Second World War as an air-raid warden, he was invited to become coach to Warwickshire. He held the position for nine years and had the distinction of coaching the side that won the County Championship in 1951. It was a unique achievement. He had played in Warwickshire's first championship side and coached the second, forty years later.

Tom Dollery succeeded him as coach and Smith took over the indoor cricket school. He was now sixty-nine, but he continued to maintain an active interest in the school until 1970.

He had by now become a revered figure in English cricket. He would watch the play at Edgbaston from the corner of the players' dining room and there were many who sought his advice. They would come to him with their batting problems and he would watch them in the middle. Then he would diagnose what was wrong and suggest a remedy. He had a wealth of experience of cricket, and of life, and he was a sensitive and highly intelligent man who had transcended the humblest of beginnings.

Mike Brearley and Geoff Boycott are among those who benefited from talking to him, and neither is a man who goes to others lightly. If Brearley has since become a guru of the cricketing world, he would testify to what he owes Smith in terms of directions of thought about the game.

Smith found no place among the biographies in *Barclay's World of Cricket*, nor was he ever one of *Wisden*'s 'Five Cricketers of the Year', but *Wisden* was able to rectify its error by making his obituary a feature article, and a fine one, by Rowland Ryder, son of the Warwickshire secretary with whom Smith had a few battles.

'Tiger' Smith died in August 1979. He was ninety-three and had been the oldest living Test player. Rowland Ryder invoked the words Smith had used about Oldfield and Lilley in describing the old warrior himself. He had 'an enthusiasm greater even than dedication'. More aptly, Ryder used the words of Field Marshal Slim to describe Smith's attributes: 'resilience, adaptability and a cheerful refusal to lie down under difficulties'.

He was a much-loved man and after his death his ashes were sprinkled over the turf at Edgbaston where they love his memory still.

There are those who, wrongly, would deny him a place among the great wicket-keepers. There are few who deny him a place among the great men of cricket.

6

Strudwick: Record Breaker
and Gentleman

'In all my career I have done nothing startling, except when I broke the wicket-keepers' record; but I have tried to play the game, have never appealed unless I felt confident and I am more proud of this than any other performance of merit.'

This passage, appearing towards the end of Herbert Strudwick's autobiography, *25 Years Behind the Stumps*, is typical of the modesty and charm of the man.

'If he appealed for a catch at the wicket, it was an *appeal*,' wrote Sir Neville Cardus, 'a question.'

'He was first of all a gentleman and a sportsman,' said Herbert Sutcliffe, endorsing the view of the *Wisden* obituary that 'no more genuine sportsman in every sense of the word, than the teetotal, non-smoking Strudwick ever took the field for Surrey'.

Herbert Strudwick had his first trial with Surrey in 1896 and he served them until 1958 when he retired from his job as scorer. For thirty years he had worked in the score-box and for thirty years before that he had kept wicket for the club.

He was born in Mitcham on 28 January 1880 and, when very young, used to take his lunch and go to watch the Mitcham club. He was a choirboy at the parish church and played in cricket matches with the other choir boys. These were supervised by the daughter of the vicar of Mitcham, Miss Wilson, and it was she who suggested that Strudwick should become a wicket-keeper. He was about ten years old at the time and was in the habit of running in from cover to the wicket to take returns from the field. It was this that prompted Miss Wilson to say, 'You ought to be wicket-keeper.' He took her advice and played in this position for the rest of his life.

His first match of importance was for Mitcham Boys against South London Schoolboys, and he did well enough to be asked to play for the South London Schoolboys in a few games at the Oval. When he was sixteen he received a postcard inviting him to go for a trial at the Oval.

He was told to go into the nets and stand behind the stumps, and he had to take the bowling of Len Braund, the brisk leg-break bowler and forcing bat who was to be discarded by Surrey within a couple of years and find fame and glory with Somerset. All went well until Strudwick tried to take a leg-side delivery from Braund and received a severe blow on the side of the head. The Surrey officials told him that he was too young and that they would offer him another trial when he was older.

They kept their word and he reappeared at the Oval two years later in 1898. This time he impressed the officials and they took him on the staff, but not before Len Braund had split the joint of the first finger of his right hand with a quicker delivery outside the off-stump.

This was the first of a series of terrible injuries that his hands were to suffer over the next thirty years. Scantily protected, they were gnarled and misshapen by the end of his distinguished career. Eventually, he sought extra protection and was one of the first to have solid leather tips inserted in his gloves for his thumbs and fingers. His method of palm protection was less orthodox. Some wicket-keepers had pieces of raw steak inside their gloves to afford greater protection for the palms; Strudwick had dampened inner gloves. When A. G. Pawson, the Oxford University wicket-keeper, asked him for advice on technique, Strudwick replied forcefully, 'You must rinse your hands in the chamberpot every day. The urine hardens them wonderfully.'

It must be remembered that adequate protection for the hands and body was developed late in Strudwick's career. Wicket-keepers wore the same pads as the batsmen and there were no 'boxes' until 1910. The first 'box' was marketed by J. T. Tyldesley, who had suffered a six weeks' lay-off after being struck in the groin, and so was created out of necessity and sympathy.

Fred Stedman, who was the Surrey wicket-keeper when Strudwick arrived, used to protect his chest with a copy of the South Western Railway timetable, and on one occasion, after he had received a particularly severe blow, he remarked to a colleague, 'I shall have to catch a later train tonight. That one knocked off the 7.30.'

Strudwick, too, took some severe knocks on the chest. He recalled one ball from J. N. Crawford which exploded from a length on the fast Oval wicket and lifted sharply so that it nearly cracked his breastbone. But it was the hands that suffered most. Jack Hobbs, who had the greatest admiration for him, said, 'He was lucky to a degree; in fact, many a time in the early days I have known that he could not sleep at night owing to bad fingers, but next day he would be taking his place at the wicket and would be going about his work as though nothing was wrong with him.' And Strudwick himself admitted that there were times when he could not sleep at night for the pain in his fingers, but he had been brought up in a hard school where the remuneration was small, and to stand down through injury could mean the loss of one's place for a season, or longer.

When Strudwick joined the Surrey staff the system at the Oval was hierarchical, with the old professionals keeping themselves aloof from the youngsters on the ground staff. The hours were long and the work was hard, but if one survived and won through to the first team, a tough battle had been won.

Strudwick played initially for the Surrey Colts, who were led by W. C. Graburn, the man who had employed him, and in 1899 he played his first match for Surrey second XI. The next year he had his first match in the first team, against the West Indies, but he did not play again until 1902 when he was in the side against W. G. Grace's London County XI. He also played against the two universities, but Stedman was wicket-keeper in the

County Championship matches except for the last of the season, against Warwickshire, when Strudwick made his debut.

In 1901 Stedman had beaten all records by accounting for 87 batsmen – 71 caught and 16 stumped – and as Surrey possessed another good wicket-keeper in Marshall, it seemed that Strudwick's chances would be limited. Throughout the winter of 1902–3, however, he practised hard with his brother, who would throw a ball at him from a short distance to both left and right for at least half an hour each day.

At the beginning of the 1903 season Strudwick shared the Surrey wicket-keeping duties with Stedman, but a 50 against Essex, which was to be one of the very rare batting successes of his career, clinched his place. It was hard on Stedman, but he would merely look at the team list and say, 'You're playing, matey' and 'Someone had to stand down for me, and you will stand down for someone in time to come.'

There was certainly some feeling among Surrey members that Stedman should have been in the side, but Strudwick's performances soon silenced all criticism. It was a wet summer and Surrey had their worst season for more than a decade, but, as *Wisden* reported, 'The one particularly bright feature of Surrey cricket last season was the development of Strudwick into one of the smartest wicket-keepers of the day.'

This was something of an understatement, for he had 63 catches and 17 stumpings in the County Championship and, in all matches, 93 dismissals – a record for a wicket-keeper which was to stand until 1911 when Huish became the first man to reach the hundred.

The Surrey attack was a pace attack, with Richardson, Lockwood, Lees and Clode bearing the brunt of the work. For the most part, Strudwick conformed to the contemporary practice of standing back to fast bowlers, but he was just as adept standing up if the circumstances demanded, and his keeping to Rushby, close up, was commented upon most favourably. Hobbs insisted that Strudwick could have stood up to all bowlers, but considered that there was more to be lost than gained by doing so, an argument put forward by Alan Knott in recent times.

Strudwick's form was so impressive that he was invited to represent the Players at the Oval, during which match he made four catches, two of them off Tom Richardson, whose last match in this series it was. At the end of the season he was invited to go to Australia as Lilley's deputy. He had, from the first, said *Wisden*, 'a touch of genius'.

In spite of touring Australia in 1903–4, he did not play in a Test match until England toured South Africa in 1909–10. Then he played in all five Tests of the series under the captaincy of H. D. G. Leveson-Gower, although he did not keep wicket in the fifth Test. In the first Test, in Johannesburg, he had three victims, one of them a stumping off G. H. Simpson-Hayward, the last of the lob bowlers, who took 6 for 43 and 2 for 59 with his underarm spin to the leg and the off.

It showed how versatile a wicket-keeper had to be in the early part of the century. When Strudwick first appeared for the Players he had to keep to the bowling of Albert Trott, and he asked Trott how he would be able to read his cleverly disguised quicker ball. 'You'll soon find it,' Trott said. It was, however, some time before Trott bowled the fast ball, and when he did, it just missed the leg-stump and hit Strudwick full toss on the foot. He hopped around in considerable pain and Trott came up to him and said, 'You found it all right, then.'

By 1911 Strudwick was at the height of his powers and kept magnificently to the bowling off 'Razor' Smith and Rushby. Smith moved the ball venomously at medium pace, and Strudwick would often take him shoulder-high standing up to the wicket. He was named as one of *Wisden*'s 'Five Cricketers of the Year', but he also received an admonition: 'Strudwick bubbles over with energy that sometimes carries him too far. I can see no advantage in his habit of leaving his post and chasing the ball to the boundary. The practice is simply the result of over-keenness, but as it does no good it ought to be checked, and

I would suggest to the Surrey captain a system of modest fines, the amount being increased for each offence.'

It is doubtful whether the Surrey captain ever took the advice of the editor of *Wisden*, for Cardus remembered Strudwick years later chasing after a hit to leg in flapping pads, flicking off his glove, picking the ball up on the run and returning swiftly and accurately. Cardus called him one of the best outfielders in the land.

The greatest quality in his wicket-keeping was his quickness of foot, and it was this speed that brought a new dimension to the art, for Strudwick was capable of taking catches in front of the wicket as well as behind the stumps. In the Surrey *v.* Leicestershire match at the Oval in 1911 he flung himself full length in front of the wicket to catch King off Smith, and the editor of *Wisden* described it as 'the most remarkable thing of its kind I have ever seen'. And *Wisden* was not given to such extravagance of language.

Strudwick went to Australia in 1911–12 as England's premier wicket-keeper, but, as already described, he lost his place to 'Tiger' Smith after one Test match and did not play for England again until the first Test at Durban in December 1913.

This was the series in which Sydney Barnes took 49 wickets with medium-pace bowling that defied all categorizing. The Tests were played on matting wickets and Strudwick reached his peak as an international cricketer. He took 15 catches and made 6 stumpings, 3 of which were made off Barnes and 1 off Johnny Douglas, to whom a modern wicket-keeper would certainly stand back.

Strudwick was thirty-nine when cricket restarted after the First World War and he had doubts as to whether he would be able to re-establish himself in the Surrey side. Captain Heath deposed him for one match at the beginning of the season, but he won his place back and kept it until the end of his career.

He went on his third tour to Australia in 1920–21, playing in four of the five Tests, all of which were lost. Dolphin kept in the fourth Test and when the sides met in England in 1921 Strudwick lost his place to George

Brown after the second Test match. It was a bad time for
English cricket, but Strudwick was to play long enough
to be part of the glory that was to come. He was forty-
one years old before he played for England in England.

Brown and Street were the wicket-keepers in South
Africa in 1922–3, and when the South African side came
to England in 1924 they were confronted by three different
keepers in the series – G. E. C. Wood, George Duckworth
and, in the last Test, Strudwick.

George Edward Charles Wood was a Cambridge blue
who had been forced to decline the offer to tour Australia
in 1920–21, Dolphin replacing him. Wood was in the
great tradition of Kent wicket-keepers and had been in
A. C. MacLaren's side which had inflicted the only defeat
on Warwick Armstrong's Australians in 1921 at
Eastbourne. Wood stood right up close to the stumps for
even the very quickest of bowlers, but his appearances
were restricted because of business and he played only a
handful of games for Kent in the 1920s.

Duckworth's time had not yet arrived, and it was Strudwick and Whysall who were sent to Australia in 1924–5.
Whysall was very much an emergency wicket-keeper, in
the Fowler or Andy Stovold category, and he played in
the last three Tests in the series as a batsman, scoring
well. Strudwick, now with greying hair, kept in all five
Tests. 'He was,' said M. A. Noble, 'one of the outstanding
successes of the tour.'

England lost the series by four Tests to one, and when
Strudwick played in the side which was victorious at
Melbourne it was the first time in eleven Tests against
Australia that he had been on the winning side.

The Australians recognized him as 'a wonder wicket-
keeper' with his efficient, quiet and unobtrusive work. He
was businesslike in all he did, walking briskly to the other
end in between overs 'as though grudging the time taken
up in changing ends, as though, in fact, he just lived for
keeping wicket'. In his collection of throws from the field,
he remained an example to wicket-keepers half his age.

One thing that disconcerted him on the tour was the
pace of the Australian wickets, which were then at their

hardest, and Strudwick had been used to standing up to all but the very quickest bowlers, but he was aggrieved to find that Tate hustled so fiercely off the Australian pitches that he had to stand back to him on occasions.

There was always the feeling that the England selectors were looking elsewhere for a wicket-keeper, that neatness, dependability and agility in the art were in themselves insufficient, and Strudwick was nearly denied his greatest moment. He kept for England in the first four Tests against Australia in 1926, but they were all marred by rain and were all drawn. For the fifth Test at the Oval, which was to be played to a finish, Percy Chapman was brought in as captain in place of Carr, and he asked George Brown to keep wicket instead of Strudwick, sacrificing the better keeper in search of a few runs. It is an equation that has never balanced.

On the eve of the match George Brown damaged a thumb and Strudwick was recalled. He surrendered only 5 byes, caught Bardsley and Mailey, and ran out Ponsford, giving 'England excellent service'. England won by 289 runs and regained the Ashes for the first time in fourteen years. It was an emotional and historic occasion and a wonderful end to Strudwick's Test career.

He played one more season for Surrey and then became their scorer. He entered into partnership with Alf Gover and, for a time, helped to run a most successful coaching school in South London. S. C. Griffith, the former secretary of MCC, remembered him with the greatest affection: 'This wonderful man and great cricketer taught me, when I was fourteen, all I ever knew about wicket-keeping at the cricket school he helped to run in South London. He was the best coach I have ever known and from that time I always numbered him among my dearest friends.'

Strudwick had a rare capacity, as Cardus noted, in that 'in a moment he would find in you your wave-length of affection'.

Sir Henry Leveson-Gower, who captained him for Surrey and England, wrote of him: 'When you walk on to a certain cricket ground and you find Strudwick behind the wicket, you feel that you will not only get full value

for your money, but you will participate in the cheerfulness that his presence always lends to the day.'

Strudwick maintained his connection with Surrey until
1958 when, at the age of seventy-eight, he retired as
scorer; but he was to live and enjoy cricket for another
twelve years.

In style, Strudwick was an orthodox wicket-keeper,
although film unearthed by David Frith of Strudwick
keeping in the indoor school would suggest that he tended
to take the ball with the fingers pointing towards it,
thereby increasing risk of injury. His stance was very close
to the wicket for all bowlers but the quickest, and, being
short, his nearness to the stumps gave him a neat,
compact, uncramped style. He was above all courageous,
determined and honest in all that he did. He was quiet,
unobtrusive, consistent and popular, and, until the arrival
of Godfrey Evans, there had been no wicket-keeper as
quick on his feet. The quickness of foot and an uncanny
sense of anticipation born of years of experience were the
keys to his success, together with a consistent concern for
his job.

Bert Oldfield recalled an incident when he and Strudwick were travelling together to play opposite each other
in a Test match at Manchester:

He was sitting with his back to the engine and I offered him
my seat, but he politely refused saying he never travelled with
his face to the engine as there was always the risk of one getting
a piece of soot in one's eye. I was struck by the wisdom, yet
simplicity of his logic, and could not but admire it, as it was
just another striking instance of the care and consideration that
some cricketers give to their welfare in the interests of the game.

When he left the cricket field in 1927 Herbert Strudwick
had taken 1235 catches and made 258 stumpings. It was
a record that was to remain unbeaten for forty years.

But it was not as a record-breaker that Strudwick is
remembered. His energy and good humour were as great
at the end of a long hot day as they had been at the
beginning. He always bubbled with exuberance. Whether
standing back or crouching over the stumps, he was a

constant threat to the batsman, and, as Leveson-Gower noted, in the gathering of terrible returns he was unequalled. It was this potential that the daughter of the vicar of Mitcham had recognized in 1890.

He had patience and the concentration to expect a catch every ball. If one expects a catch, he believed, one will make a stumping easily enough. He never appealed unless he was certain that the batsman was out, considering it unsporting to do otherwise, and he never did anything intentionally unsporting in the whole of his life. This was the reason he was so popular among spectators and other players.

'It is because of such men as Hobbs and Strudwick,' wrote Leveson-Gower, 'that the professional cricketer of today is held in such high esteem.'

And there are those today who, when you talk to them of wicket-keepers, will say, 'Ah, but you see, I saw Strudwick.'

7

Oldfield
and the Australian Tradition

In 1919 the Australian Imperial Forces team toured
England as an appetizer for the resumption of Test
cricket. They were a strong side, six of whom were invited
to return to England with the full Australian side of 1921.

They met Surrey at the Oval. Kelleway, who was
leading the Australians that day, approached Strudwick,
as the doyen of wicket-keepers, and asked him if he would
go to the nets and have a look at their young keeper, a
lad named Bert Oldfield, and offer him some advice.

Strudwick watched Oldfield for about ten minutes. He
took the ball cleanly and was very quick in all his
movements. The England keeper turned to Kelleway and
said, 'I can't teach him anything – in fact, he's more able
to teach me.' Within a year Strudwick and Oldfield were
on opposite sides in a Test match.

In the opinion of most good judges, Bert Oldfield was
to become the best wicket-keeper that the world has seen.
He was the first man to reach 100 dismissals in Test
cricket, and in all he was to catch 78 and stump 52
batsmen in his fifty-four Test matches. Twenty-eight of
his victims were off the bowling of Clarrie Grimmett.

'Tiger' Smith considered that he was everything a
wicket-keeper should be: quiet, alert, calm and nearly
faultless. His footwork was excellent and his movements
so smooth that he was never out of position. He stood up
to the stumps far more than most keepers of his period,
and he took the bowling of Grimmett, Mailey and
O'Reilly, none of them easy, without any trouble.

Les Ames says simply, 'He was the best I ever saw.'

Yet it is quite remarkable that Oldfield ever became an international wicket-keeper. He was born in Alexandria, Sydney, and educated at Forest Lodge and Cleveland Street schools, but his first experience of wicket-keeping was with a church team in the Western Suburbs Junior Cricket Association in Sydney. The church was to shape his life ever afterwards, moulding his way of living and winning him the nickname of 'the gentleman in gloves'. For many years he was vestryman at St Andrew's Cathedral, Sydney.

He was ever mindful of his debt to those early days in the church team:

In most Junior Cricket competitions in Australia the matches are played on a concrete wicket covered with green coir matting, a surface from which the ball frequently rises sharply and awkwardly. It is the sort of surface on which a slow leg-break bowler can make the ball spin viciously, and in those Junior days no doubt I missed a lot of chances, but there is equally no doubt that by the hard way I learnt a lot. It was hard-won experience which was of tremendous help to me later when I graduated to the Glebe District Cricket Club in the Senior competition where all the games are played on the easier turf wickets.

It was in 1914, when he was twenty years old, that Oldfield first played for Glebe in the City and Suburban Competition. He made 84 in his first match on the Sydney Domain and was tempted to forget wicket-keeping and concentrate on his batting, for he had captained Cleveland School as a batsman and a bowler, and he won his way into the third-grade side solely as a batsman.

He continued to make runs in the third team, but one day, when the usual wicket-keeper failed to arrive, he volunteered to go behind the stumps and was so impressive that he was asked to stay in the position.

He played only two more games for the third team before being chosen as wicket-keeper for the first XI, missing the second team altogether.

His first great memory was of catching Syd Gregory at Wentworth Park, Sydney, and he then began to practise

with Test players like Bardsley and Kelleway. But the
First World War broke out and in September 1915 he
enlisted in the army. He was with one of the first contin-
gents to go to Egypt and after a few months his unit was
transferred to France, where he immediately saw front-
line service.

A corporal in the 15th Field Ambulance, 15th Brigade,
he was one of those caught in the heavy German
bombardment of the Ypres Salient at the end of 1917. A
shell burst near his stretcher squad in Polygon Wood and
three of his friends were killed. Oldfield was buried under
debris and when he was finally dug out he was unconscious and close to death. He suffered from shell-shock
for more than six months and was invalided to Gloucester
in 1918.

When he had finally recovered he was posted to the
Headquarters Staff in London, and there he joined the
Wattle Club, playing club cricket against such sides as
North Middlesex, Beckenham, East Moseley and Merton,
where he hit his first century in any type of cricket.

The Australian Imperial Forces had two sides in the
field in England in 1919 and Oldfield began with the
second of these; but first-choice wicket-keeper Ted Long
received a gash on the face from Jack Gregory in the
match against Middlesex at Lord's and that evening
Herbert Collins went round to Oldfield's dingy lodgings,
close to the team's headquarters in Horseferry Road.

Collins did not know Oldfield either by sight or name
and asked him if he were the chap who kept wicket. When
Oldfield said that he was, Collins asked him to play
against Oxford University the next day. Oldfield
protested that he was not good enough for that class of
cricket, but Collins said that he had had good reports of
him from other soldiers, and as a result Oldfield got on
the train to Oxford with whatever cricket gear he could
muster tied in a bundle.

He took four catches in the match, and by the end of
the first over Collins recognized that here was a great
wicket-keeper. After the match Ted Long, who had been
watching, went to Collins and said that, having seen

Oldfield, he realized that he would no longer be needed; but he stayed with the side as reserve keeper.

The next match was at the Oval and it was here that Strudwick saw Oldfield play for the first time and passed his judgement.

Oldfield saw Jack Hobbs score 205 not out in that match, and in the next few weeks he was to have his first sight of players like Hitch, Tennyson, Hearne, Mead, George Gunn, 'Tiger' Smith and Woolley.

He learned much from Collins, who had succeeded Kelleway as captain after a disagreement and who was responsible not only for Oldfield's development, but also for encouraging Jack Gregory and Johnny Taylor. What impressed Oldfield most about Collins was his thinking on the game. He would sit at a player's bedside on the night before a match and discuss plans for the next day, or would even greet them in the morning with ideas and thoughts that he had had. For the rest of his life, Oldfield was to be a studious wicket-keeper, reinforcing his natural athletic ability and intuition with meticulous observation of the game and its players.

The Australian Imperial Forces team played in South Africa on their way back home, and then played Victoria, Queensland and New South Wales on their return to Australia. Oldfield had 14 dismissals in these three matches and his reputation grew. At Melbourne it was reported, 'Oldfield kept wicket splendidly, catching Liddicut off a leg-glance in remarkable fashion', and at Brisbane, 'Oldfield added greatly to his reputation behind the wicket'.

He did not play in the Sheffield Shield in 1919–20, however, for Hanson Carter, Australia's wicket-keeper, was captain of New South Wales. Oldfield shared the duties with Carter for New South Wales in 1920–21 and played in the first three Test matches against England, Carter keeping in the last two. When the Australians came to England in 1921 Oldfield came as reserve to Carter and played only in the fifth Test.

Carter had succeeded Kelly as Australia's wicket-keeper in 1907 and, although unorthodox, he had his great days. Oldfield had been impressed with him as a young man, particularly by his neatness and his quickness in stumping, but, on closer observation, he realized that Carter's was a unique style which would not be good to imitate. He would stand some 4 feet away from the stumps, making it necessary for him to take a step forward in order to bring off a stumping and increasing the angle of deflection at which a catch would come to him; but he squatted low, had clever footwork and good anticipation, and so met with much success.

'Sammy' Carter, who was an undertaker by profession, was unquestionably a character. He would arrive at matches in a two-wheeled carriage drawn by a pony, and sometimes in a hearse. He taught Oldfield the wisdom of applying eucalyptus to the rubber palms of his wicket-keeping gloves.

Oldfield impressed everyone with his wicket-keeping at the Oval in his first Test in England, for he showed no worries in taking the bowling of Gregory, McDonald and Mailey, and conceded only 1 bye as England scored 647 runs. He played in one of the three Tests against South Africa at the end of the tour of England, and then he took over completely as Carter passed from the scene.

When Gilligan led the England side to Australia in 1924–5 Oldfield gave what is reputedly the finest display of wicket-keeping ever seen in a Test series. In the third match he took the vital catch to dismiss 'Tich' Freeman off Mailey and win the match for Australia by 11 runs, and in the fourth Test he gave a remarkable display, stumping Hobbs, Woolley, Chapman and Whysall, and catching Gilligan in a match which England won by an innings. The stumpings were made off three different bowlers – Mailey, Kelleway and Ryder – and the stumping of Hobbs off Ryder became legendary.

Hobbs had scored three centuries in the preceding Tests and looked set for a fourth, having scored 66 out of an opening partnership of 126. He played forward in an attempt to leg-glance a delivery from Ryder which was unexpectedly quick and rose head-high. Hobbs overbalanced and lifted his back foot fractionally. Oldfield gathered the ball and, in an amazing movement, flicked off a bail. Not only had he had to take the ball in front of his face, but on the leg-side. In his own words, it was the greatest stumping of his career, and there were 261 of them: 'Ryder was bowling from the Members' end and, anticipating the altered direction of the ball because of the natural slope of the Melbourne cricket ground, and also noting that he was swinging the ball sharply to the on-side, I was in the position to take the ball, and after the fractional second in removing the bails Umpire Crockett upheld my appeal.'

The studious care and dedication that went into this single stumping are an example of Oldfield's art. But he wasn't yet finished with Jack Hobbs, whom he admired above all other batsmen. In the fifth Test he caught Hobbs in the first innings and stumped him in the second. If any should doubt that the ability of a wicket-keeper can affect the course of a game, he should ponder on Oldfield's catch in that first innings. Australia had been dismissed for 295, the lowest first innings of the match score in the series. The match was at Sydney and Gregory bowled the opening over. Oldfield recalled:

The first ball of his opening over from the Paddington end altered its direction towards the leg-side on account of the wind. I noticed that the second ball had the same tendency, but the third, perfectly straight, was patted back by Hobbs to the giant bowler.

Then came the fatal ball, fatal for dear old Jack! Pitched just outside the leg-stump and with the assistance of the wind, it swung well away to the leg-side, aided by the firm glance from Hobbs's bat; but having those first two deliveries as a guide, and seeing that the fourth ball was pitched on the leg-side, I anticipated its course by covering a greater distance, and as soon as I heard the snick I stretched my arms full length while in my stride, probably 4 or 5 yards wide of the wicket, and brought off a catch, which certainly thrilled me and brought the spectators as a man to their feet.

It was Hobbs's only 'duck' in five trips to Australia, and Macartney described it as the greatest catch he ever saw.

It should be emphasized that Oldfield was still on his feet when he took the catch. For him, anticipation made the full-length dive superfluous.

He had 18 victims in this series, 8 of them stumpings, and it was in the fifth Test that he began his association with the great leg-break bowler Clarrie Grimmett.

It was not in dismissals alone, however, that Oldfield's value as a wicket-keeper could be measured. He had an electrifying effect on the team around him. He was the hub of a superb fielding side, and could lift a team by his example. When Jack Gregory became lethargic Oldfield would stand right up behind the stumps to the fast bowler. Feeling stung by the action of his wicket-keeper, Gregory would renew his vigour.

Oldfield's keeping was as impressive as ever in the fractured series in England in 1926, and he was named one of *Wisden*'s 'Five Cricketers of the Year'.

It was when he was playing his twenty-eighth consecutive Test match for Australia at Adelaide in 1933 that he ducked to a ball from Larwood and was hit on the head. He was carried from the field unconscious and taken to hospital. Fingleton and Woodfull had been hit earlier in the same innings of this match which brought the 'body-line' crisis to its head. Oldfield did much to diffuse the situation when he insisted, on recovering, that the injury had been his own fault and that he should not have ducked into the ball. In later life he and Larwood became firm friends.

He was back in England in 1934 and toured South Africa in 1935–6, where he made keeping wicket to the eccentricities of Fleetwood-Smith look a simple task.

When the Australians came to England in 1938 it was without Oldfield and Grimmett, and these omissions caused much controversy and, many advocated, prevented them from winning the series. In a controlled criticism of the selection of the side, 'Third Man', *The Cricketer*'s correspondent in Australia, commented:

Everyone must feel a pang of regret at the absence of Oldfield whose polished and undemonstrative wicket-keeping has kept

Australia so strong in this department for sixteen years. Although still capable of brilliant things – including those catches off leg-glances – this urbane and popular cricketer was sometimes below the exalted standard he has set, but I am not prepared to accept a few blemishes in one season as proof that his powers have waned materially.

So Oldfield's Test career ended at Melbourne in March 1937, when he caught Barnett and Allen, and stumped Voce off O'Reilly. He had not conceded a bye in either innings.

Neither of the wicket-keepers chosen for the 1938 tour – Barnett and Walker – had ever played Test cricket and, sadly, Walker was never to become an international. He was injured on the tour and killed in action in the Second World War.

Bradman must have sighed for Oldfield at the Oval in 1938 as Hutton batted on for hour after hour to reach his 364. Before he had achieved his first century he went forward to a ball from Fleetwood-Smith which spun past him while he was well out of his ground; but it spun past Barnett, too, and the chance was not to come again. Barnett was a good wicket-keeper and a most likeable man who later settled in England, but he was no Oldfield.

When war broke out in 1939 Oldfield was forty-five and, obviously, his career was at an end, but he maintained that enthusiasm beyond dedication, with which 'Tiger' Smith credited him, to the very last. This enthusiasm manifested itself in his mode of practice. In his schooldays he had always carried a tennis ball with him which he would constantly bounce against high walls and on the pavement to sharpen his reflexes. As a man, in the sports store in Hunter Street, Sydney, which he owned, he insisted that his staff should throw items to him so as to keep him alert and keep his eye in. His dedication was taken to extremes, for it was said of him that during the season he would neither read nor go to the cinema for fear of straining his eyes.

Impeccably dressed, on and off the field, his style was to crouch low as the bowler began his run, with his heels firmly on the ground. Balance, timing, composure and poise were his trademarks, and his colleagues nicknamed him 'Cracker' as a tribute to his quickness of movement. For fast bowlers he would always stand at a point where he could take the ball chest-high. He would have been scornful of the modern method of taking the fast bowlers so far back that often the keeper is taking it on the ground.

Scrupulously fair, he appealed only when he knew a batsman was out, and his appeal was always a quiet, apologetic inquiry, never a raucous demand. It was said that umpires came to look at Oldfield when the Australian slip cordon exploded in appeal and they were undecided. If Oldfield had remained silent, they gave 'not out'. Strudwick never forgot that once, in a Test match, he appealed for a catch behind against Oldfield which was given 'not out', but the batsman, knowing that he had touched the ball, walked. It has not been a common occurrence in the years since then.

Robertson-Glasgow remembered an incident when he did not walk and Oldfield's courtesy shamed him for years to come:

Batting just above the extras for Oxford, I snicked a ball from Hendry that broke back and kept rather low. It hit the leg edge of the bat and also the pads, and Oldfield caught it in both hands near the ground. The appeal was turned down. At the end of the over Oldfield quietly said. 'You did hit that, didn't you? Ah, I thought so. Oh, it doesn't matter about the decision. It was the catch I was thinking about.' So am I, still.

The catch was in 1921, and Robertson-Glasgow wrote this piece in 1943.

Oldfield's hands suffered over the years. He did not put steak on the palms as some did, but wore two pairs of inner gloves. Perhaps he did not use steak because he shared Wally Hammond's opinion of the practice. When asked what was the most difficult time for fielding slip, Hammond replied, 'On a blazing hot afternoon at Melbourne when the steak in the keeper's gloves had gone off and the stink was unbearable.'

Oldfield thought much about wicket-keepers' gloves

in later years and modelled them from his experience, supplying Keith Andrew and Bob Taylor, among others.

Sparing time from his work in manufacturing sporting goods, Oldfield took several Australian schoolboys' teams overseas, and one of his most remarkable achievements was to promote cricket in Ethiopia, where he became a great favourite of the Emperor, Haile Selassie. In addition, in 1976, just before his death, he flew to Hong Kong with his old friend and adversary Harold Larwood to open a new cricket ground.

He had come a long way from the back streets of Sydney, and he made many friends and gave much joy on the journey.

8

George Duckworth
and the Cult of Personalities

Oldfield hit six centuries in his career, which indicates
that he was a more-than-useful batsman, but it was as a
purist wicket-keeper, unostentatious and composed, that
he was chiefly recognized. In effect, he was the last of a
line, for only Keith Andrew since has really approached
him in style and unspectacular efficiency. After the
Second World War wicket-keepers began to change in
style, and different demands were made of them.

One other purist remained down in Sussex until the
outbreak of the Second World War. He stood just over 5
feet tall and so, of course, was called 'Tich'. His real name
was Walter Cornford, and Cardus numbered him among
the best five wicket-keepers he ever saw. Brian Johnston
counts it a privilege to have seen him play.

Cornford was born on Christmas Day 1900 and
succeeded George Street as the Sussex wicket-keeper when
the latter was killed in a motorcycle accident in 1924. He
stood right over the stumps to the bowling of Tate and
Gilligan, and was splendidly neat and compact in all he
did.

He earned Tate, his closest friend, and Gilligan several
wickets with his agile stumpings, but his most treasured
memory was of the occasion when he stumped Jack Hobbs
twice in a match off Wensley, and held five catches in the
same match off Maurice Tate.

His opportunities in Test cricket were very limited,
initially because of Strudwick, ultimately because of
Duckworth and Ames; but he did play in the inaugural
Test match against New Zealand at Christchurch in 1930

and in the other three Tests of the series. He had the doubtful distinction of conceding 31 byes in New Zealand's innings of 387 in the fourth Test, but this was mainly due to some erratic bowling on an uncertain wicket.

While the MCC side under A. H. H. Gilligan, which Cornford accompanied, was playing Tests in New Zealand, another, under the Hon. F. S. G. Calthorpe, was playing Tests in the West Indies. Such was the strength of England in the early thirties.

Cornford played for Sussex with consistent success until the outbreak of the Second World War, after which he coached at Brighton College. He reappeared for Sussex in one match in 1947 when neither 'Billy' Griffith nor his deputy was available. The game was against Essex at Brentwood at the beginning of June, and Cornford, right behind the wicket as always, stumped Dodds off opening bowler James Cornford (no relation) and then stumped Horsfall, who was making his debut, off George Cox. In the second innings he caught Tom Pearce off Charlie Oakes and finished with a flourish when he stumped Bill Morris off fast-medium left-hander Doug Wood to end a ninth-wicket stand of 111. It was a fitting postscript for a brilliant wicket-keeper.

Cornford's career coincided with that of George Duckworth, and although many considered Cornford a better keeper, it was Duckworth who was to win fame and most of the honours.

Duckworth was born in Warrington on 9 May 1901. He was educated at Warrington Grammar School and lived all his life in the town in which he was born.

In 1922 he was invited to go to Edgbaston for a trial, but Lancashire were interested to secure his services and he joined their staff, making his first-team debut in 1923 and quickly establishing himself as the regular keeper.

It was a good time to have joined Lancashire. MacDonald, the great Australian fast bowler, had qualified to play for them by 1924 and Cecil Parkin was in his prime. For the three years 1926–8 Lancashire were to win the County Championship, and their deeds and characters were to be chronicled by Neville Cardus, who was to win acclaim as the first and greatest of cricket journalists. As has been discovered since, Cardus was not always historically accurate in his writing, but he immortalized the Lancashire players of the period and none more so than George Duckworth.

Indeed, Cardus maintained that he himself was the first player ever to be stumped by George Duckworth at Old Trafford: '. . . it was a so-called friendly match, and when I missed the ball and Duckworth shrieked his appeal and swept up all the bails and the stumps, I felt as though I had been sandbagged.'

Duckworth's rise was meteoric. In July 1924, after one full season, he was in the Players side which overwhelmed the Gentlemen at Lord's, and a month later he was in the England team for the rain-ruined Test against South Africa at Old Trafford.

He was not taken to Australia in 1924–5, Whysall being used as Strudwick's deputy, an ominous portent of future selections when batting prowess was to be deemed more important than accomplishment behind the stumps, but he was in the England side against the West Indies at the Oval in 1928. This was the third of a three-match series in which Harry Smith of Gloucestershire kept in the first Test and Harry Elliott of Derbyshire kept in the second.

The year 1928 was one of cricket's golden years and Duckworth had a share in it. He caught 77 and stumped 30 batsmen. His 107 dismissals would have been a new wicket-keeping record but for a young man from Kent who accounted for 121 batsmen in the same year. Nevertheless, they both went to Australia and it was Duckworth who played in all five Tests.

He was now firmly settled as one of the great characters of the game. Cardus wrote of him:

Men often tell us by their physical appearance what they do for a living. Lawyers look legal; colonels look belligerent; ostlers look like horses about the mouth; and wicket-keepers look like nothing on earth but stumpers. George Duckworth was made by nature to sit close to the ground; he bends nicely, and his voice would have been wasted in any occupation but the one he adorns so perfectly.

Duckworth's method of appealing was famous from the start. It was a demand, a decision, rather than a question, and it punctuated the game several times every hour. 'It was not so much an appeal,' said John Marshall, 'as an assertion. He was directing the umpire in his bounden duty and he wanted his decision to be known far beyond the boundaries of Stretford, to say nothing of echoing up and down the Warwick Road line.' Invariably, the shrill and loud appeal was accompanied by the right hand being lifted on high as if in answer to his own supplication. His was the triumphant crow of the cock. It was once said that only one man appealed more often, and that was Dr Barnardo.

The way in which he appealed only complemented his physical attitude to the game. Duckworth was swift in his movements, belligerent and vocally demonstrative. He bubbled, and when he stumped, it was almost in a frenzy.

By general consent, he was at his best when standing back, and he stood reasonably far back to MacDonald, off whom he took some marvellous diving catches on the leg-side. He never hindered the slips, but he was always actively and aggressively present.

He had, wrote Cardus in *World of Cricket*, 'omnipresent hostility'.

This aggression was the quality that Cardus had noted some thirty years earlier:

The power exercised over a great batsman by a great hostile wicket-keeper is not estimated by half on the score-sheet; it is not merely the catches and the stumpings that tell the tale; the aggressive presence of a Duckworth prevents a batsman from attempting strokes which would be safe enough if the wicket-keeper were only a more or less passive accessory after the bowler's act. Duckworth is attacking from behind as directly and violently as the bowler is attacking from the front.

Duckworth was not the most stylish of keepers – Cardus accorded that privilege to Oldfield and to Henry Martyn, who stood up to the fierce pace of Knox, Brearley and Kortright – but he was rapid, accurate and ever vigilant.

Oldfield, so pure and effortless in all he did, was somewhat bemused by Duckworth when the Lancastrian arrived in Australia in 1928–9. He took to his rich, warm character, but his style of wicket-keeping raised doubts in his mind.

Duckworth was immediately popular in Australia with his reddish, boyish face and his native wit and good humour. He was energetic and enthusiastic on the field, establishing an immediate personality. He became a centre of interest among Australian cricket followers because he was so unlike his predecessors and his style was so very different.

Oldfield described Duckworth in action:

It was not an unusual sight to see Duckworth, never still for a moment, trying to roll up his sleeves with his gloved hands, at the same time casting quick glances at the slips and then at the bowler. A moment later he would be bringing off an amazing stop from a wide delivery. In so doing, however, he frequently revealed a weakness in footwork as, in endeavouring to take such a ball, he would finish up full length on the ground with outstretched arms, having just managed to stop it.

With Duckworth came the extrovert, leaping and diving wicket-keeper. He founded a new dynasty.

He played in the first four Tests against South Africa in 1929 and Les Ames made his Test debut in the fifth. Duckworth was back to keep in all five Tests against Australia in 1930, but these were to be his last against the old enemy and his selection for the side was not without much argument.

The two teams arrived at the Oval for the final Test having won one game each and drawn two. This was, of course, Bradman's first tour. R. E. S. Wyatt replaced Percy Chapman as captain for the final Test and the selectors took the unprecedented step of taking two wicket-keepers to the Oval and not deciding until the last minute which one was to play. They settled on Duckworth, whom Wyatt considered to be the better keeper, and Ames was omitted.

It was a fateful decision. Wyatt's selection as captain had been controversial and he and Duckworth bore the brunt of the criticism when Australia regained the Ashes by an innings victory.

Wyatt won the toss and England made 405 which, as they had been 367 for 5, was a disappointment. When Australia batted, Woodfull and Ponsford began with a stand of 159, but Duckworth dropped the former when he was 6 and the latter when he was 23 and 45. Woodfull went on to score 54 and Ponsford 110. Worse was to follow, as reported in the *Sydney Sun*. 'When he was 82 Bradman gave a difficult chance to Duckworth, but the little wicket-keeper made his third miss of the match. Bradman cut a ball from Hammond only a few inches off the ground, but Duckworth fumbled it and then dropped it.' Bradman scored 232.

Cardus argued that Duckworth created 'chances' by his acrobatics that others would never have anticipated, and there seems to be some justification for this view when one considers that the *Sydney Sun* accused him of three, not four, misses; but Wyatt and others were adamant that but for Duckworth's lapses, England might well have won. All wicket-keepers have bad matches. Unfortunately, Duckworth's worst was in front of a full ground at a crucial Test match involving the greatest run-maker the world has ever seen.

His Test career was not over, however. He went to South Africa in 1930–31 and kept wicket in the first three Tests before he was injured. His deputy there was the man who was his deputy at Lancashire, Farrimond, who had won the place much as Paul Downton won his trip to Pakistan as an 'unknown' a few years ago. Duckworth went to Australia and New Zealand in 1932–3, the 'body-line' tour, but he was by then understudy to Les Ames and kept only in the second match in New Zealand as a compensation. When Ames was injured he played in one Test against South Africa in 1935, and, in that peculiar series of selections, Farrimond also kept in one Test.

Duckworth's last Tests were the three against India in 1936. When he caught Wazir Ali off 'Gubby' Allen at the Oval it was his 60th dismissal, 15 of them stumped, in twenty-four Test matches.

He made his last trip to Australia as Ames's deputy in 1936–7, and at the end of the 1937 season he retired, although there was still much cricket left in him. He had always been willing to stand down to give opportunities to Farrimond and now he stepped aside for the younger man.

Duckworth became a journalist, but war brought an abrupt end to this career. He then spent time in hotel management and farming before returning to journalism, and broadcasting, after the war.

He acted as baggage man and scorer on three MCC tours and managed three Commonwealth sides to India. These were positions for which his genial personality was eminently suited.

He was a good judge of a player and had an intelligent understanding of the game, but above all, as John Marshall said, 'No Lancashire player has been so abundantly Lancashire.' He served the club as well on the committee as he served it as a player, and for many, Old Trafford has never been quite the same since the day his cry of 'Howzat?' was heard for the last time.

9

Les Ames:
the Great All-rounder

There must be something in the air of Kent that breeds wicket-keepers, urges them to flourish and to surpass all others in the art.

In the beginning there was Jenner and Wenman, and then there was Tylecote, who played for England and hit 400 in a school match. At the start of this century there was Huish, the first centurion, and he handed over to Jack Hubble, who was always pressed by the amateur, Wood, the best amateur wicket-keeper since Martyn. The future was to bring 'Hopper' Levett, Godfrey Evans and Alan Knott. But it was Hubble's successor, Leslie Ethelbert George Ames, who, in the opinion of many people, was the best of them all and the best that is ever likely to be seen.

Les Ames committed the crime of being too talented. People found it hard to accept that here was a cricketer who was good enough to play for his country both as a batsman and as a wicket-keeper. There have been wicket-keeper-batsmen since, but there has never been another who could have represented his country equally consistently as one or the other. On top of this, he made wicket-keeping look so easy just at a time when people were being taught to believe that it had to be flamboyant.

Oldfield, when commenting on Duckworth's style of going full length to make a stop that would have the crowd roaring, made the following comparison: 'I have noticed that Ames was able to achieve the same result and still retain his poise whilst taking similar bowling.'

Ames was so quiet and unnoticed in all he did, changing ends between overs with no sign of hurry, yet arriving as quickly as others who displayed more histrionic vigour. He reflects now: 'Perhaps, I was too self-effacing. I didn't do myself justice. I should have been more showy, but I could never see the need.'

'He was wonderful,' says 'Hopper' Levett, who spent most of his own career in Ames's shadow. He continues:

He stood up to everything. The game has changed today. There is no devilment, only containment. There is no comparison today. They are backstops, magnificent catchers, not wicket-keepers. In Les's time if you didn't stand up to medium pacers, you weren't considered a keeper. The art of a wicket-keeper is seen in how well he takes slow bowling, how he can pull off a stumping. Some were not so good at taking the slow stuff, but Les was an all-round wicket-keeper. He could take the lot.

Les Ames was born in Elham, between Folkestone and Canterbury, on 3 December 1905. He was educated at Harvey Grammar School, Folkestone, and, encouraged by his father, a useful club cricketer, he displayed early enthusiasm for cricket. At the age of thirteen he won his place in the first XI and kept it for the next four years. He prospered in a moderate school side, scoring a century against Dover County School and, on odd occasions, keeping wicket.

He also played occasionally for the Elham village side, but when he left school he went to live with his cousin in Brabourne, near Ashford, to work in the grocery business and learn the trade.

He joined Smeeth, a local village club, and soon won a reputation as a hard-hitting batsman. He recalls:

Above all else, I used to love fielding. I was a quick runner and I got more fun out of fielding than anything else, but I saw what a mess was being made of the wicket-keeping and now and again I used to go behind the stumps because I couldn't bear to see the job done so badly; but I never enjoyed it as much as fielding.

Home from the Sudan, A. G. Pawson, father of Tony Pawson, remembers playing in a club match at Rye and noting the excellence of the wicket-keeper on the other side. So impressed was Pawson, an Oxford blue, that he recommended the young man – Leslie Ames – to Gerry Weigall, the Kent County coach, a rich character.

Weigall was already aware of Ames's promise, but the young man was told that he was not quite up to standard when he first went to Tonbridge for a trial. In the coming weeks, however, his batting for Smeeth blossomed and, following an innings of 185 not out, he was asked to play for Ashford against Kent Club and Ground.

Gerry Weigall was captain of the Club and Ground side and was sufficiently convinced by the quality of Ames's innings of 46 to ask him to play for the Club and Ground side in their next match. It was Weigall who impressed upon him the need to do something else as well as bat. He believed that all young cricketers should be 'double barrelled', for there were not too many Jack Hobbses about who could rely on their batting ability alone. Ames's father was a left-arm bowler, but his son had no aptitude for bowling. Weigall asked if he was any good behind the stumps and Ames told him that he had kept a few times at school and on odd occasions for Smeeth. 'Good,' said Weigall, 'then you can keep wicket today.' And that was in his first match for Kent Club and Ground, against Hythe.

On a turning wicket he kept to spinners Hever and Hearn, and collected three catches and a stumping. He kept wicket occasionally for the rest of that season, and then he was asked to join the Kent staff for the 1925 season.

When he arrived at the beginning of the season he was told that as Povey, the reserve keeper, was no longer on the staff, he would be considered Hubble's deputy.

In July 1926 he made his debut in first-class cricket, but not as a wicket-keeper. He batted at number five and scored 35 as Kent beat Warwickshire by an innings. He took four catches in the match, two in the deep and two at short-leg. The two in the deep were off 'Tich' Freeman.

They were the first entries in the score-book which brought together the names of Ames and Freeman. There were to be 357 more in the following ten years.

Les Ames played in the next match, against Nottinghamshire, also at Tunbridge Wells, and then returned to the second XI for the rest of the season. It is strange that, although he kept wicket in neither of his first-team outings, *Wisden* wrote: 'Much is expected of Ames, the reserve wicket-keeper, who, making two appearances, displayed promising form, not only in that capacity, but also as a batsman.'

He was in the side for the first match of the 1927 season. It was against Worcestershire and was the first county match to be played at Folkestone. J. B. Higgins was stumped Ames, bowled Freeman in the first innings, becoming the first of the 259 batsmen who fell in this manner. There was never a more lethal combination in the history of the game.

Ames says that he was very nervous when he kept to 'Tich' Freeman in that first match, for he had only kept to him in pre-season practice before this, when Frank Woolley had given him much advice on how to read the ball. He soon settled down, however, and found no difficulty in spotting what was the googly, what was the top-spinner and what was the normal leg-break:

I couldn't understand later why batsmen got in such a mess against 'Tich' because I always knew what was coming and could read him, but most of them never could. I once played against him in a Festival match, but he never bowled me the googly. He thought it would be a waste of time. He was the best spin bowler I ever saw, along with Laker, and it was he who made me into a wicket-keeper.

He had a catch off Beslee and another stumping off Freeman in the same match, and he also scored 90.

Ames played in twenty-eight of Kent's thirty matches that season, although Hubble, who retired at the end of the year, kept wicket in six of them. He hit the first of his 102 centuries at Southampton on Whit Monday and by the end of the season had scored 1211 runs. He had also confirmed his outstanding ability behind the stumps and been selected for two Test trials, but this was only a foretaste of what was to come in 1928.

That year, 1928, was an *annus mirabilis*. May was damp, but after that the sun shone, and runs and wickets were everywhere. Ernest Tyldesley, Sutcliffe, Mead, Hendren and Woolley all passed 3000 runs, and fourteen other batsmen passed 2000. Douglas Jardine averaged 87.15 and 414 centuries were hit during the season. MacDonald took 190 wickets for Lancashire, and Jupp, Tate and Parker all passed the 150 mark. 'Tich' Freeman became the first, and one would assert the last, bowler to take 300 wickets in a season, and Les Ames, too, had a place in this historic year.

He hit 1919 runs and scored his first double century. It was against Surrey at Blackheath in what was once a most famous annual fixture. Moreover, he caught 69 and stumped 52 batsmen in the season for a record 121 dismissals.

In 1911, when he was thirty-eight years old, Fred Huish, dark, neat and elegantly moustached, had accounted for 100 batsmen, and two years later he had established a new record with 102 victims. Huish's outstanding achievement had been at the Oval in August 1911, when he had caught one and stumped nine Surrey batsmen in the match. Ironically, it was Herbert Strudwick's benefit match.

Ames caught nine in the match against Oxford University in 1928 and was to catch five and stump four in the match against Sussex a year later, but in recording dismissals one must always consider how much a wicket-keeper owes to the bowlers. Les Ames has told of his debt to Freeman. Huish was aided by Blythe and Woolley, and when Ames talks of the wicket-keeping of Arthur McIntyre, whom he greatly admired, he speaks of McIntyre's reliance on Laker and Bedser:

You get your hands knocked about a bit when you are standing up, and the off-spinner is the most difficult to take because the ball is coming into you most of the time and leaving you blind for a fraction of a second. Tom Goddard gave me more problems than anyone else I kept to and I would not have liked keeping to Laker. That is why I thought McIntyre was so good in the way that he took Laker and Alec Bedser standing up. They made him into a top wicket-keeper.

However much he owed to Freeman, Ames's record in 1928 was phenomenal, and one cannot help but feel sorry for George Duckworth, who also established a new record that year with 107 dismissals, only to find himself trailing by 14 at the end of the season.

When he had completed his second season in county cricket, Les Ames was named one of *Wisden*'s 'Five Cricketers of the Year' and was on his way to Australia with the MCC team. He had twice passed 1000 runs and had established a new wicket-keeping record. He was just twenty-three years old.

There was still a reluctance in some areas to believe that a player could be so good in two departments of the game. As well as being a fine batsman, there was the deceptive ease with which he kept wicket, almost a nonchalance, although astute judges noticed that he got down very low when standing up and that his rhythm was easy. He rose with the ball and it was all a question of perfect timing, which was why it looked so easy. Ironically, in its assessment of him, *Wisden* was worried because he had had insufficient practice in standing back to fast bowlers.

Ames did not play in any of the Test matches in Australia in 1928–9, but he made his international debut in the fifth Test against South Africa in 1929, ironically 'Tich' Freeman's last, and played in all four Tests in the West Indies the following winter. As already noted, Duckworth returned for the series against Australia in 1930.

By that time, Ames had surpassed his previous record. In the 1929 season he caught 79 and stumped 48 batsmen and so established a record of 127 dismissals which, like Freeman's 304 wickets, is unlikely ever to be beaten. In the same season he scored 1795 runs with five centuries.

He says now that the most difficult thing about wicket-keeping is to maintain concentration, especially when having hit a few runs. Young keepers today – David East, Parks, Richards – endorse this view. Les Ames's powers of concentration must have been unparalleled.

By 1931 he was England's first-choice wicket-keeper, playing in all three Test matches against New Zealand. In the four Test matches in the West Indies he had hit two centuries, and in the first Test match against New Zealand at Lord's, going in at number seven with the score 129 for 5, he hit 137. He and 'Gubby' Allen put on 246 for the eighth wicket, a record for all Test cricket. Ames was the first England wicket-keeper to score a hundred in a Test in England. In all, he was to score eight Test hundreds, including in 1934 the first hundred by a wicket-keeper in England v. Australia Tests. If one is looking for comparisons, 'Patsy' Hendren scored seven centuries in his fifty-one Tests. Ames played in forty-seven Tests and scored well over 2000 runs at an average of more than 40.

He played in the inaugural Test against India in 1932 and then went to Australia for the 'bodyline' series. Much has been written about this series, some fact and some fiction, and most of it concerns the trials and tribulations that the Australian batsmen suffered at the hands of Larwood and Voce; but little has been said on the effect that leg-theory bowling had on the fieldsmen and wicket-keeper.

Ames, it must be remembered, had raised doubts because of his lack of practice in taking fast bowling standing back, and now he was asked to keep to the fastest bowling in the world aimed on or around the leg-stump.

Certainly, Ames was not in as much danger as the batsmen, but he had to adapt to the new line of attack and new field placement. His stance had to re-adjust to cover the leg-side, and for most of the time he could not get a full view of the ball until it had passed the batsman. Quietly and efficiently, again almost unnoticed, he adjusted to this new style of bowling.

Oldfield's one criticism of him was that in standing up

to medium-pace bowlers, he did not cover the line of the good-length ball on the leg-side, preferring, as Oldfield put it, 'to feel for it blindly'. Oldfield maintained that, in adopting this style, it was not possible to bring off certain catches which could have been achieved using the orthodox method. Ames did move across to take short-pitched balls on the leg-side, so, in effect, it was a case of choosing the method which suits. As he had four dismissals off the brisk medium pace of Wally Hammond during the series, two of them stumpings, it must be assumed that Ames's method worked well.

His attitude to leg-theory bowling was a reasoned one. He saw it as a style that had evolved as a necessary curb to the cool, calculating run-machine that Bradman had become, but he hoped that not every bowler would adopt this mode of attack, for it would mean an end to classic batting and the disappearance of the loveliest shots – the off-side strokes.

In 1932 Les Ames took 100 dismissals for the third time and 64 of them were stumpings. As with his 127 dismissals in 1929, neither his feat of a century of dismissals in three separate seasons, nor his 64 stumpings in a season is ever likely to be equalled. It is interesting to note that the last wicket-keeper to make 100 dismissals in a season, Roy Booth of Worcestershire in 1964, did so with the aid of only nine stumpings. Times change.

For Ames, the heights had still not been reached, and in 1933 his wicket-keeping, 'ripened by his experiences in Australia, looked still more impressive'. His batting outshone that of all others in the country save Hammond and Hendren. He hit a century in each innings against Northamptonshire at Dover, 295 against Gloucestershire at Folkestone, and double centuries against Warwickshire at Tonbridge and for the Players against the Gentlemen at Folkestone. His aggregate for the season was 3058 runs, and he was top of the Test batting averages against the West Indies with an average of 83.50. It is interesting to note now that the bowler he considered to have troubled him most in the whole of his career was Learie Constantine.

In the third Test match at the Oval he gave a magnificent display of wicket-keeping, mainly to the eccentric leg-breaks and googlies of 'Father' Marriott who, playing in his one and only Test match, took 11 for 96. Ames had two stumpings and a catch off him, three catches off Clark, and two off Nichols. He conceded only 1 bye in the match.

In 1934 he was fourth in the first-class batting averages and played in all five Tests against Australia, his wicket-keeping again being exemplary. In the first innings of the final Test, however, he was forced to retire hurt with a strained back, a warning for the future.

This match had seen the recall to Test cricket of Frank Woolley at the age of forty-seven, and when Ames was unable to keep wicket in the second innings it was Woolley who went behind the stumps. He caught Chipperfield and conceded 37 byes, a record for Test cricket.

Woolley's terrible performance as wicket-keeper, even allowing for the fact that he was, incredibly, doing the job for the first time in a senior match at the age of forty-seven, was a counter to Ames's self-effacing argument that any good fielder could do the job competently. Woolley, as a slip fielder, was on a par with the great Wally Hammond, of whom Ames says, 'Wally was a natural, brilliant fielder – everywhere. He could have kept wicket as well as anyone. He had quick reflexes and that's all you should need.' But it isn't all you need. Ames was a natural wicket-keeper; it came so easily to him that he could not always understand why others did not find it just as simple a task. Many great artists feel the same way.

In an interview, George Bernard Shaw once said, 'When I was a boy the one thing I never wanted to be was a great writer because I was a great writer.' At first it sounds like arrogance, but it is the truth. Ames could never see what all the fuss was about with regard to wicket-keeping because he was, by the gift of nature, one of the very greatest of wicket-keepers.

He had begun the 1934 season shortly after an operation for appendicitis and he ended it with a strained back.

The following year was one of strange selections when he played in four of the five Tests against South Africa, but was included at Lord's simply as a batsman, Farrimond keeping wicket. In the Test in which he did not play, Duckworth kept wicket. Ames caught three and stumped two in the final Test and scored 148 not out, sharing a fifth-wicket stand of 179 with Maurice Leyland.

Ames had one of his poorer seasons in 1936, but he won the first of his two Lawrence trophies by scoring the fastest century of the season, in 68 minutes against the Indians at Folkestone. He was always a hard-hitting batsman with a swiftness of foot that allowed him to punish spinners severely, and he was never afraid to hit the ball over the field.

The back trouble recurred in August 1936, and although he was passed fit to make his third trip to Australia, he suffered from further trouble as soon as he got there. He recovered in time to play in all five Tests, however, and accounted for 15 batsmen in the series; but the back trouble was to niggle at him for the rest of his career.

He played his last two Tests against Australia in 1938. They were the first two of the series and he was later kept out of cricket by a broken finger which was sustained in the Lord's Test. He kept in all five Tests during the tour of South Africa in 1938–9, but the back trouble, first diagnosed as lumbago and then as a slipped disc, reasserted itself. It was brought about by the sudden movement necessary in bending quickly to retrieve balls from the field, and Sir Pelham Warner was adamant that his injury was caused by poor throwing. Ames did not keep wicket at all in 1939 and his Test career was at an end. None before, nor since, has ever remotely approached his standard as a wicket-keeper and batsman.

International selectors have since tried to force leading batsmen into the role of wicket-keeper. There was a time when Kanhai and Walcott were used as wicket-keepers, with unhappy results, and New Zealand had a chastening experience when they tried to use 'Jock' Edwards, a forcing, pleasing batsman, as a Test wicket-keeper, a position for which he was all too obviously unsuited.

Some have maintained that it is impossible to play a long innings and then to sustain concentration behind the stumps. At Brentwood at the end of May 1934 Les Ames hit 202 not out against Essex in 2 hours 50 minutes. Then he went out and caught Pearce off Valentine, Cutmore off Watt, and stumped Ashton and Taylor off Freeman. In the second innings, when Essex followed-on, he caught Pope off Wright and finished the match with two stumpings off Freeman.

It was at first argued that it was only the spin of Freeman which gave him his victims and made him look a good wicket-keeper, but then he went to Australia and, in the fiercest bowling series ever witnessed, kept to Larwood, Voce, Allen, Bowes and Hammond. At Lord's, in 1937, he kept for the Players against the Gentlemen and left viewers stunned by his display. The Players' attack consisted of Jim Smith, Arthur Wellard, Wally Hammond, James Langridge and Tom Goddard. James Langridge bowled only 6 overs in the match and did not take a wicket. Ames had eight dismissals and took chances off all the four main bowlers. He had two stumpings off Goddard, who was 'the bowler who gave me most trouble'.

When war broke out Ames joined the Royal Air Force and rose to the rank of Squadron Leader. He captained the RAF in several exciting games at Lord's and thrilled everyone with his batting.

After the war he continued batting for Kent, but, perhaps by some decree of the gods of cricket, kept wicket for them only once, against Middlesex at Canterbury on 11 August 1950, in the second innings after Godfrey Evans had hurt his right hand. He had no luck behind the stumps, but he was soon at the wicket when Kent, having been set to make 237 to win in 2½ hours, had lost Fagg for 0. He shared thrilling partnerships with Hearn and Tony Pawson – at one time 85 runs came in 35 minutes. He scored 131 out of 211 in 2 hours and Kent won by 4 wickets. It was the hundredth hundred of his career, and the crowd and the Middlesex players gave him the warmest of congratulations.

The following winter he captained the Commonwealth team in India, Pakistan and Ceylon, but on returning to England he was attacked by fibrositis. His health broke down in the first match of the season, against Nottinghamshire at Gillingham, and he did not play again. The trouble was diagnosed as a slipped spinal disc. Had he remained fit, he would have been named as captain of Kent for the 1952 season.

He was elected a member of the MCC and a life member of Kent, serving them as secretary and manager and leading them to one of the great periods in their history. He was the first professional cricketer to become a Test selector, a task he undertook with great understanding and compassion. A wicket-keeper with a cricketing brain can be of invaluable assistance in the planning of a side, and Les Ames has an abundance of wisdom. Ted Dexter says of him: 'He is one of the few people with whom a discussion on cricket remains firmly based on fact not fiction, on opinion not prejudice.'

To sit with him in the Kent committee room and simply to listen to him is an education, for the man, as thrilled by Kent's success today as he was by his own, is so balanced and calm in assessment. Sometimes, however, he will explode: 'Look at that,' he will say. 'The best wicket-keeper in England standing back to a bowler of Woolmer's pace.' Then he will soften. 'He's a great keeper. The game has changed. The one-day game changed things. Slips disappeared. The wicket-keeper stood back because he had to take everything. It is easier and more profitable. They do all sorts of acrobatics now. I could never have done those.'

'That's because he didn't need to,' says 'Hopper' Levett.

10

'Jock' Cameron
and the South Africans

At the beginning of the century 'Dick' Lilley was impressed with the wicket-keeping of two South Africans: Ernest Halliwell and Percy Sherwell.

Halliwell was born in Ealing in fact, and played once for Middlesex and once for the Gentlemen against the Players at Hastings in 1901. His father, R. Bissett Halliwell, had kept wicket for Middlesex in his early days, so the art was in the family blood.

Ernest Halliwell went to the Gold Coast and India before settling in Barbeton in the Transvaal. He came to England with the South African teams of 1894, 1901 and 1904. He was reared on the matting wickets in South Africa where, he advocated, it was better to stand up to everything, although he felt that in England there were more opportunities to take catches if one stood back.

Lilley supported this view: 'Wicket-keeping on matting is different altogether from keeping wicket on turf. The ball comes at a good pace, and is much easier to take. But on the sticky wickets in England it is infinitely more difficult, and requires very careful watching.'

Halliwell's great strength was his keeping to the fast bowling of J. J. Kotze. Kotze, a Boer farmer from Western Province, was one of the fastest bowlers that South Africa ever produced, and he and Halliwell seemed to have a perfect understanding.

A strongly built man with a dark moustache, Halliwell introduced the practice of having a piece of raw steak in his glove when keeping wicket. This was no doubt inspired by his partnership with Kotze.

92

Halliwell was succeeded by Percy Sherwell, who captained South Africa in all thirteen Test matches from 1905 to 1911, when they relied upon the great googly quartet of White, Faulkner, Vogler and .Schwartz. Sherwell was also an excellent batsman, but it was the way in which he kept to the googly bowlers that won him the greatest admiration. 'This class of bowling needs a lot more watching than any other,' wrote Lilley. 'Nothing could possibly be finer than the way in which he took them, and his stumping of Hayward in both innings in the second Test match at Leeds was magnificent.'

Lilley was always impressed by Sherwell's neat style, and he certainly had the very highest opinion of him:

I consider that Mr Sherwell was a better wicket-keeper to medium-pace bowling than Mr Halliwell; but the latter, to my mind, never had a superior to fast bowling. I have seen Mr Sherwell do some particularly smart work in stumping off the googly bowlers, and it was always executed in that artistic style which must appeal to anyone who knows what wicket-keeping is.

Sherwell was slighter than Halliwell, with a Kitchener-style moustache that dominated a clear-eyed face which invariably wore a kindly smile. He was a natural athlete and became his country's tennis champion in 1904. He was a South African Test selector from 1907 to 1924.

In a conversation with Lilley in 1907 on the eve of that year's series, Percy Sherwell expressed great optimism about the rising generation of cricketers in South Africa. He could not have known that there was a two-year-old boy in the Cape who was destined to be one of the world's very great wicket-keepers. His name was Horace Brackenridge Cameron and he was born at Port Elizabeth on 5 July 1905.

'Jock' Cameron was educated at Hilton College, Natal, and at Jeppe High School, Johannesburg. His interest in cricket began early and his ability as a wicket-keeper was recognized at school and encouraged. He won a place in the Transvaal side as wicket-keeper and as a hard-hitting batsman, and played against Lionel Tennyson's side in

1924–5. He scored his maiden century in 1927 and made his Test debut the same year playing in all five Tests against England.

He came to England in 1929 and immediately impressed all who saw him. He began with a century against Worcestershire and caught six and stumped one in the match against Somerset. In the second Test at Lord's he was struck on the head by a ball from Larwood which rose fiercely from a length. It was a terrible blow and he was carried from the field unconscious. He was out of cricket for three weeks and missed the third Test at Headingley – the only Test he missed in his eight-year international career.

Cameron's nerve and determination seemed unaffected by the blow he'd received at Lord's, but it probably had a more significant influence on future events than many realized at the time.

He captained South Africa in the final Test against England in 1930–31, and then led the side in Australia and New Zealand; but he was not the first, nor the last, to find the task of batting, keeping wicket and captaining too onerous. His wicket-keeping maintained its usual high standard, but his batting fell away. There is every reason why a wicket-keeper should also be a good captain, for he sees the game more closely than most and is directly concerned all the time; but so deep is the concentration needed for his particular task that he cannot give the wider thought to the game that is often required. When Alexander captained the West Indies the game slowed to a snail's pace, and very few other keepers have made a success of the job. Cameron was happy to serve as vice-captain to Wade on the 1935 tour of England.

This was the great South African triumph. They beat England at Lord's, their first Test victory in England, in the only match of the series that was not drawn, and so they won the rubber. In all matches they were beaten only twice, and those defeats came in late August when the party was obviously tiring.

Cameron played a historic part in the victory at Lord's. South Africa were 98 for 4 when he came to the wicket.

The correspondent of *The Cricketer* described his innings as memorable:

Then came Cameron to play a magnificent innings. He hit three 6s, the first to square leg, off a full pitch of Verity's, into the Mound Stand, the second into the Grand Stand, also to square-leg off Langridge, and the third into the pavilion seats off Mitchell. He scored *58 out of 60 in half an hour* by beautiful stroke play all round the wicket. We have seldom, if ever, seen a batsman who hits a ball so hard and so far with so little apparent effort. Cameron has, of course, fine wrists, but he must also possess uncommonly strong forearms. The crowd roared with delight at his superb cricket. In the end he fell, after the tea interval, to Nichols, who had just gone on with the new ball, and it is safe to say that his innings will be remembered for many a long day. He was at the wicket for an hour and fifty minutes.

He made 90. It was to be his highest score in Test cricket.

Nor was his part in South Africa's victory over. In the first England innings he caught Nichols, in the second, when he did not concede a bye, he caught Hammond, and he finished the match by stumping T. B. Mitchell off the leg-spinner Balaskas.

A week before this match he had hit 103 not out against Yorkshire, who were to win the County Championship that year. In the course of that innings he scored 30 in 1 over off Hedley Verity – 4, 4, 4, 6, 6, 6. Verity took 211 wickets that season at 14.36 runs each.

In his last innings in England Cameron hit 160 in 140 minutes against H. D. G. Leveson-Gower's XI at Scarborough. He was not to play another first-class innings. The team left England at the end of September, and Cameron developed enteric fever and died on 2 November 1935. He was eight months short of his thirty-first birthday.

His batting ability has been mentioned, but fierce as his attacking stroke play was, he was no slogger, and it is as one of the world's great wicket-keepers that he is remembered. In his time he was ranked on a par with Oldfield and Ames. The latter thought him magnificent:

'He was a charming man. He stood up to nearly everybody and his keeping to Bell, who could be very quick and erratic, was marvellous.'

Cameron had, of course, learned his craft on the matting wickets in South Africa which, as already described, if consistent, did present their own problems. He was particularly adept in taking the bowling of 'Buster' Nupen. He bowled fast-medium round the wicket and a mixture of off-cutters and leg-cutters that were lethal on matting, but Cameron took him with ease.

Never dropping below the highest standards, Cameron took the ball naturally, without fuss or flourish. He appeared to have a hypnotic effect upon the ball, drawing it to him. He was exceptionally quick and, in that undermentioned part of a keeper's work – taking returns from the field – was quick to determine the length of the throw and adjust to gather with ease.

Indeed, *ease* was the word most readily used about his keeping. His style was once described as 'the perfection of ease and rapidity without unnecessary show', and his incredibly quick stumping was likened, in one memorable phrase, to the 'nonchalant gesture of a smoker flicking ash from a cigarette'. During his last season in England he took 35 catches and made 21 stumpings, and in the final Test at the Oval, when only 6 English wickets fell, he caught Bakewell and Wyatt, and stumped Hammond and Leyland. It was a fitting end to a great, but all-too-brief career.

Above all, Cameron was a charming man with a strong personality. In its obituary *The Times* wrote of him:

As a cricketer his record speaks for itself, and as a man it is hard to think of anyone who could have been better liked. He combined all those qualities of courage, modesty, generosity, and cheerfulness which instinctively made themselves felt on the field of cricket, and also off it, to all those who were privileged to know him and who immediately recognized the influence of the man.

By one of those rare chances, 'Jock' Cameron died within a month of the Rev. A. P. Wickham, who had allowed

John McCarthy Blackham: 'the Prince of Wicket-keepers'

Bill Storer: he stood up to the fastest bowling

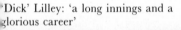

'Dick' Lilley: 'a long innings and a glorious career'

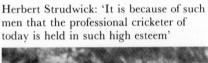

Herbert Strudwick: 'It is because of such men that the professional cricketer of today is held in such high esteem'

'Tiger' Smith: (*left*) towards the end of his playing career, 1928; (*right*) the inspiration of Warwickshire — coach to the championship side, 1951

Oldfield stumps C.F. Walters at Worcester, 1930

Bert Oldfield: impeccable and honest in all he did

George Duckworth: Old Trafford has never been quite the same since he retired

The greatest wicket-keeper-batsman the world has ever seen. Les Ames attempts to stump Rhodes (Yorkshire) off 'Tich' Freeman at Tonbridge, 1932

Members of the South African team arrive in England, 1929: (left to right)
C. Vincent, H.G. Deane, R.H. Catterall, H.B. Cameron and A.L. Ockse. South
Africa have never had a greater keeper nor more popular man than 'Jock' Cameron

Wicket-keepers at rest. Don Tallon (left) and Gil Langley (right) chat to Australian
manager George Davies (centre), May 1953

Alan Knott: a magnificent attempt to catch Jeff Thomson in the second Test against Australia at Perth, 1974. The bowler is Chris Old

Evans in typical tumbling mood as he attempts to catch W.E. Jones, Kent v. Glamorgan, Gillingham, 1950

Wasim Bari catches McCosker, Leeds, 1975

Brian Taber, New South Wales and Australia, a greatly respected keeper

Knott himself falls victim to Deryck Murray

Knott breaks the wicket, but Mallett has just got home

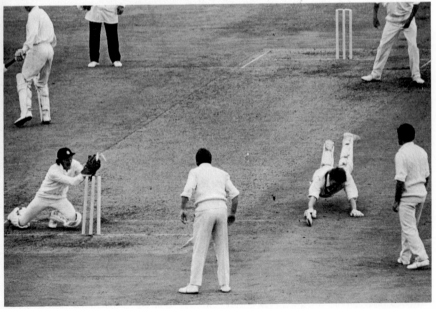

Bob Taylor: unquenchable enthusiasm

Syed Kirmani attempts to stump Rodney Hogg

Gilbey's Golden Glove Award for the Wicket-keeper of the Season, 1983, goes to David East of Essex. The presenter is the great Godfrey Evans

no byes when keeping for Somerset as Hampshire scored 672 for 7 at Taunton in 1899, a record that has never been surpassed.

Cameron's spiritual successor in the South African side was John Waite, who became the only one of his countrymen to play in fifty Test matches, breaking all records as a wicket-keeper. He had a record 26 dismissals against New Zealand in 1961–2, having had 23 dismissals against them eight years earlier, and there was rarely a match in which he did not account for several batsmen. In his fifty Tests he caught 124 and stumped 17 batsmen and throughout his career he had 427 catches and 83 stumpings.

Like Cameron, he was a quiet, self-effacing keeper, but he tended to stand back more in the changed circumstances that prevailed in the 1950s and early 1960s, and he made some spectacular diving catches. As a batsman, he was more dour than Cameron, with a restricted backlift and a sound defence, but he scored four Test centuries and a total of twenty-three in the whole of his career.

He, in turn, was succeeded by Denis Lindsay, whose father had played three Tests when South Africa came to England in 1947. Denis Lindsay was a batsman in the Cameron mould. He first came to notice when he hit Bill Greensmith, the Essex leg-spinner, for five successive 6s at Chelmsford in 1961 when playing for Fezelas.

In the series against Australia in 1966–7 he hit 606 runs, which is a record for a wicket-keeper, and also took 24 catches, which remains a record for a five-match rubber. Rodney Marsh's 26 catches were made in a six-match series.

Lindsay's most remarkable performance in this series was in the first Test at Johannesburg. He took six catches in the first innings, a Test record, and then hit a maiden Test century, 182 in 247 minutes. Two catches followed in the second innings to bring him a unique wicket-keeping record. South Africa won by 233 runs, their first home victory over Australia. The match also saw the Test debut of Brian Taber – a sensational one, with seven catches and a stumping.

The South African tradition is now being maintained, albeit in isolation, by Raymond Vernon Jennings, a young keeper of international standard.

Halliwell, Sherwell, Cameron, Waite, Lindsay and Jennings: it is a formidable list, and claims are forwarded as to the pre-eminence of each of the men on it; but it is Horace 'Jock' Cameron alone who was recognized as one of the greatest wicket-keepers of all time.

Sir Pelham Warner, who saw more wicket-keepers than most, mentioned Cameron in the same breath as Blackham, Lilley, Strudwick, Oldfield and the other immortals. Few would disagree that he deserved a place in that company.

11

Don Tallon:
Master Craftsman

When the Australian side to tour England in 1938 was announced there was much criticism that Oldfield had not been selected, and there was equally fervent criticism that a young man named Don Tallon was not to make the trip. He was then twenty-two and, in the opinion of many, was the best wicket-keeper in Australia. He was also a hard-hitting middle-order batsman who had numbered, among many fine innings, one of 193 for Queensland against Victoria at Brisbane in February 1936, a week before his twentieth birthday.

Donald Tallon was born at Bundaberg on the Queensland coast. His father was a cricket-lover and a useful slow bowler in inter-city matches. The father infused his four sons with a love of the game, and for Don that love bordered on fanaticism.

His father rolled a pitch in the back-yard and from a very early age the boys would practise there from first thing in the morning until last thing at night. Often the games would continue into the evening when, with furniture pushed back, they were contested in the living room or kitchen.

Don's most frequent companion in these practices was his elder brother, Leslie William, who was to play nine Sheffield Shield games for Queensland and become noted as a great cricket humourist. 'Bill' bowled leg-breaks, and young Don's wicket-keeping prowess was obviously sharpened by keeping to them.

He was lucky in that when he went to North Bundaberg State School he was coached by Tom O'Shea, a former inter-state wicket-keeper. O'Shea recognized the boy's outstanding ability and Don was in the school side at the age of seven. When he was thirteen he was Captain of Queensland Schoolboys, and a year later he was playing top-grade cricket.

Tall and slim, tanned and hardened by his long apprenticeship in the Queensland sun, Tallon attracted the attention of the State selectors. He had been seen at the Country Week Carnivals which were held in Brisbane, and his ability behind the stumps won universal admiration. In these weeks he kept to Eddie Gilbert, the spectacular Aboriginal fast bowler. Gilbert bowled off only four or five paces, but his very long arms and his swing in delivery generated a pace which Bradman said was the fastest he ever faced. There were doubts about the legality of Gilbert's action and his right arm swung in such a blur that keeping wicket to him could not have been easy, but the teenager from Bundaberg seemed to have no problems with him at all.

In February 1933, a week before his seventeenth birthday, Tallon kept wicket for Queensland Country XII against the MCC touring team at Toowoomba. He stumped Herbert Sutcliffe off H. Poon, was bowled by Larwood for 2, and conceded only 5 byes in the MCC's first innings of 376. The following season he made his debut for Queensland in the Sheffield Shield. He played in the match against Victoria at Brisbane in December and conceded only 6 byes in an innings of 542. More significantly, he had his first dismissal in first-class cricket when he caught Ponsford off Oxenham.

Tallon was considered too young to take on the southern tour, but when Queensland returned to play South Australia at Brisbane in January, he was in the side. He dismissed Tobin twice, caught off Oxenham in the first innings, and stumped off the same bowler in the second. He was now established as Queensland's wicket-keeper for the rest of his career.

In 1936–7 he had two catches and a stumping against MCC and, in all, had 22 dismissals in the season, in addition to finishing top of the Queensland batting averages and being their leading run-scorer. He played for Don Bradman's XI against Vic Richardson's XI in a match which, as well as being a testimonial for Bardsley and J. M. Gregory, was in the nature of a Test trial, and he acquitted himself well.

There was no sign of any loss of form the following year as he took 11 catches and 6 stumpings in Queensland's six matches, two of which were ruined by rain, but he was not selected for the England tour.

His omission from the party was greeted with a sense of bewilderment in Queensland. His response was emphatic. In the opening match of the 1938–9 season, when Queensland outplayed New South Wales in Brisbane, he held four catches and made four stumpings. When Queensland went down to Sydney two months later he equalled the world record that had been set up at the Kennington Oval in 1868 when Ted Pooley of Surrey had caught eight and stumped four Sussex batsmen. Tallon caught nine and stumped three to equal the seventy-one-year-old record. Nor was he yet finished with world records, for in Queensland's last match of the season, against Victoria at Brisbane, he caught three and stumped four in the first innings. At that time seven dismissals in an innings was a feat that had only been accomplished by Farrimond, Price and 'Tiger' Smith. It has been equalled eighteen times since, and beaten once.

His season's haul was 21 catches and 13 stumpings in the six Sheffield Shield matches, and he also hit 115 against South Australia. Incidentally, Tallon was injured in this match and could not keep wicket in the second part of the South Australian innings. There is no question that he would have come to England in 1942 as Australia's leading wicket-keeper, but because of the Second World War, that tour never took place and Tallon was robbed of six years' Test cricket.

For a time it seemed as though his Test career would never be launched. He joined the army at the outbreak of war, but he was invalided out with a ruptured stomach ulcer in 1942. This was to trouble him throughout the rest of his career until he had a large section of his stomach removed.

When cricket was resumed in Australia in 1945–6 there was unanimity in the view that Tallon was the best wicket-keeper in the world. His Test debut was a strange one in that he did not realize he had made it until two years later. Australia sent a team to New Zealand in 1945–6 under the leadership of W. A. Brown. One match was played in March 1946 against New Zealand, at Basin Reserve, Wellington, but it was not accorded Test status until 1948. Australia bowled out New Zealand for 42 and 54, and Tallon's first Test victim was Cowie, stumped off Bill O'Reilley who was, in fact, playing his last Test match.

It was when Wally Hammond's team went to Australia in 1946–7 that the cricket world recognized Tallon's brilliance as a wicket-keeper. To the speed of Lindwall and Miller, the spin of Johnson, Tribe and McCool, and the somewhat quicker left-arm spin of Ernie Toshack, he was faultless. His understanding with McCool, the leg-spinner, suggested telepathy. He had 16 catches and 4 stumpings in the series which, at the time, broke all existing records.

His one mishap was to dislocate a finger in the second Test match, but this did not hinder him in hitting 92 in the second innings of the third Test, when he and Lindwall put on 154 in 87 minutes. Like his wicket-keeping, his batting was stylish.

He kept in the series against India in 1947–8 and then made his first trip to England. It occurred ten years later than most people felt it should have done and he was now thirty-two.

He was instantly recognized in England as one of the very greatest keepers that had been seen there. He had studied the art thoroughly and been greatly helped by his predecessor, Bert Oldfield. At 5 feet 10½ inches, he was tall for a keeper, but his balance was perfect. He would fold himself almost double on his haunches. His concentration was intense, and he remained quite still while judging line, length, flight and movement, only rising to take the ball with that precision of timing that is the essence of style.

There was a paradox in his keeping, for although he was, for most of the day, totally unobtrusive and without flourish or flamboyance, his speed was rapier-like, and when a chance presented itself – a split-second stumping or a diving catch – it was accepted with lightning zest and accompanied by a strident appeal. He was like a sleeping tiger, and when he seemed to be dozing he was equally menacing. There was a frightening aggression in his wicket-keeping which reflected the corporate spirit of that great Australian side of 1948. Jack Fingleton said that he had never seen a wicket-keeper to equal him in speed. Tallon was slightly deaf, which earned him the nickname 'Deafy' from his team-mates, and often he could not hear snicks from the bat, but he was not a wicket-keeper who relied on hearing; he watched everything.

In the third Test of the 1948 tour, at Manchester, he missed Denis Compton twice in his innings of 145 not out. One chance was wide to his diving right off Lindwall, a chance that few other wicket-keepers would have even attempted, and the other was off the last ball of the day from Johnson. Tallon's keeping throughout had been so absolutely top-class that people only marvelled that he was human. It was later revealed that he had damaged the little finger he had dislocated the previous year, and as a result he missed the fourth Test.

The injured finger had not prevented him from catching Emmett of Gloucestershire off the first ball he received from Lindwall in the second innings. It was a dazzling catch. The ball went very wide away to Tallon's right, but, diving full length, he took it one-handed close to the ground. It was an appetizer for an even greater catch that was to be made in the fifth Test when he returned after injury.

The victim of this catch was Len Hutton. He had opened the England innings and was the only batsman to reach double figures. England were 52 for 9 and Hutton was on 30 when he attempted to leg-glance Lindwall. It was a legitimate shot, firmly struck, but Tallon flung himself to his left and held the ball close to the ground in his left hand as he fell. It was described separately as 'extraordinary', 'miraculous' and 'the catch of the season'.

But it must not be thought that Tallon was by nature an ostentatiously acrobatic wicket-keeper, for he was quite the opposite, consistently taking the ball neatly and cleanly. Acrobatics were for those occasions when nothing else would suffice.

In one respect he resembled Strudwick, for he would shed a glove and sprint down to fine-leg to recover a ball which would then be returned quickly and accurately.

Jack Fingleton felt, however, that Tallon missed a number of chances as the 1948 tour progressed. He said that he suffered from sore hands, and he had noticed in Australia that his form deteriorated as the season advanced. Tallon's hands certainly showed no signs of wear and tear and have been severally compared to the hands of a pianist and of a violinist. But in spite of these late-season lapses on Tallon's part, Fingleton still considered him to be the greatest wicket-keeper he ever saw. *Wisden*, while not given to such extravagances, named him as one of their 'Five Cricketers of the Year' in 1949.

When Freddie Brown took the MCC side to Australia in 1950–51 Tallon played in all five Tests against them. He dealt with the mystery spin of Jack Iverson as effortlessly as he dealt with every other bowler, but there were signs that a great Australian side was on the wane. Bradman and Barnes had gone, and the victorious side of 1950–51 could in no way compare with the side of 1948, especially when one considers that the opposition provided by England was appreciably weaker.

Tallon himself had declined and Fingleton's comment on the changing place of the wicket-keeper in the game is interesting:

I don't know that the life of a stumper in Tests nowadays is a happy one. Slow bowlers, who give them the chance to do their best work, are out of favour. There is reason to think that the main attack in Test cricket now is at the leg-stump with fast- and medium-paced bowling, and the stumper is nearly always working off his blind spot. Whatever the cause, Tallon fell below his best but he was still our best man in Australia by a long way. One trouble with Tallon was that he had set such a high standard in the two previous series.

He was still the best in Australia, as Fingleton says, and there were no arguments when he was named as first-choice wicket-keeper for the tour of England in 1953.

There was an uncertainty about his keeping in the run-up to the first Test that was perhaps only discernible to the keenest students of the game. He kept in the first Test match at Trent Bridge and caught Peter May and Godfrey Evans. They were his last dismissals in Test cricket, for Gil Langley replaced him for the rest of the series. Tallon had been seen to fumble and there was a feeling that he had lost his rhythm. Such things had not been known before.

Tallon himself was acutely aware of the fact that his glories were behind him. He played a sparkling innings of 54 not out in Queensland's opening match of the season against New South Wales when he returned to Australia, but he surrendered the keeper's gloves to Peter Burge halfway through the game and announced his retirement from first-class cricket.

He did, in fact, play in one more match, keeping wicket for Morris's XI against Hassett's XI in Hassett's testi-monial match in Melbourne. He stumped Neil Harvey off Richie Benaud, his last gesture from behind the stumps.

Quick, brilliant, stylish, never wavering in concentra-tion, Don Tallon's Test career was all too brief. Establi-shing himself in the Queensland side before he was twenty, he had not played in a Test match before he was thirty. The war cheated him of years of development, achievement and more greatness. Strangely, he had never seen a Sheffield Shield match until he played in one, but from that very first game he set himself the highest of standards.

12

The Australian Heritage: Langley and Grout

The standard of Australian Test batting and bowling suffered a serious decline in the 1950s, and it was hard to believe that Ian Johnson's mediocre team of 1956 was only eight years away from Bradman's supermen of 1948. In one respect, however, the side had lost little. Langley, if not Tallon's equal, maintained a standard of excellence that had come to be expected from Australian wicket-keepers.

Langley, who played eleven seasons of Australian Rules Football and is now Speaker of the South Australian State Parliament, was a wicket-keeper of ample proportions. His ruddy face, burly physique and cheerful disposition gave him the attributes of a Dickensian character. They were characteristics, however, which tended to hide his tremendous powers of concentration.

He was neither as stylish as Oldfield, nor as razor-sharp and quick as Tallon, but he was a most effective keeper whose anticipation helped him to reach in two strides deliveries for which others would go sprawling. His style was uniquely his own. He would squat with his right foot flat and his left heel raised. His gloves would be in front of his knees and not resting lightly on the ground in the manner of most keepers. His appearance would quickly become untidy with his waistband sagging below his midriff and, inevitably, his shirt flapping at the back. Once more, the style and the fashion obscured the great ability.

He had no family tradition of cricket and, like so many, no formal instruction in the art of wicket-keeping. He took it up at the age of twelve when he was at school and liked it, but then, he has always given the impression that he likes life and people. He is a most popular man.

He joined Sturt Cricket Club and was given a few hints by Vic Richardson, but his technique was essentially self-taught and unstudied.

When Tallon withdrew from the tour to South Africa in 1949–50, Gil Langley was chosen as Ron Saggers's deputy, and when Saggers could not play against the West Indies in the first Test of 1951, Langley came in for his international debut and created what was then a record for a newcomer, with three catches and four stumpings in the match. In the five Tests in the series, he had 21 dismissals, which equalled the Test record of Herbert Strudwick.

With Tallon back, Langley was expected to be reserve for the 1953 tour of England, but he took over after the first Test and was recognized as Australia's number one wicket-keeper.

He was injured in a Sheffield Shield match in 1954–5 when the ball that bowled Ron Archer of Queensland ricocheted on to Langley's forehead and cut deeply. This caused him to miss the third Test against Len Hutton's England side, and Len Maddocks, his deputy, did so well that he was retained for the last two Tests and for the first against the West Indies in the Caribbean. But Langley's sensitive understanding of his bowlers won him back his place and he had 13 catches and 7 stumpings in four Tests.

At Lord's in 1956 he caught eight and stumped one batsman to establish a Test record of nine dismissals in a match. It is interesting to note that he also dropped Peter May shortly before lunch in the second innings.

Langley missed two Tests in that series through injury and he was off the field for more than an hour in the fifth Test after being struck on the head by a ball from Archer, but he had 19 victims out of the 44 wickets lost in the three Tests in which he played, an unprecedented percentage of success by a wicket-keeper. In total, he played nine Test matches against England and had 35 catches and 2 stumpings, and in all his Tests he averaged four dismissals a match, a very high rate of success which surpassed all his precedessors and contemporaries. Ironically, he was kept out of the third and fourth Tests when he strained tendons in his left hand while fielding in the deep against Glamorgan.

He played against Pakistan and India after the tour of England in 1956. In the Test against Pakistan in Karachi, which was played on matting and which saw Pakistan beat Australia for the first time, he caught Zulfiqar Ahmed off Lindwall to give the great fast bowler his 200th Test wicket.

On his return to Australia he decided that it was time to retire from first-class cricket. He chose the match against New South Wales in Adelaide in mid-December as his farewell match. He took two catches as New South Wales reached 454. South Australia were forced to follow-on 265 runs behind and were crumbling badly at the second attempt, when Gil Langley went in and scored 100 before he was stumped, appropriately, off Richie Benaud. The New South Wales team joined the crowd in cheering him off the field. A big bundle of fun had gone from the game.

When Australia next put a side into a Test match, in South Africa in 1957–8, the wicket-keeper was Arthur Theodore Wallace Grout.

Wally Grout was born in Mackay in North Queensland in 1927. He was the natural successor to Don Tallon for state and country, although it took him some time to establish himself in both sides. Like Langley, he was not as neat as Oldfield, nor as quick as Tallon, and like Langley, he was an immensely popular man, regarded by all as kind and generous.

Sir Donald Bradman placed Tallon above all other wicket-keepers, but he found Grout's resemblance to Tallon in style and method quite remarkable: 'I don't know whether Tallon was an inspiration to Grout or a model which he copied, but without doubt their glove work was very similar. They had the same basic footwork, the same "swoop" on the snick, the same inevitability on holding a chance, and even the same air of intent.'

Grout was educated at Brisbane State High School, but his most important grounding was with the combined primary schools team which played in the Brisbane 'C' Grade competition. He was as much a batsman as a wicket-keeper, and it was as a batsman that he played some of his first state games.

He hit his first century when he was playing as an opening batsman in an army match, and at that time he was something of a brash youngster. He played for South Brisbane just after the war and was noted for his fondness for a bet and his habit of trying to engage the batsmen in conversation. He would shout the odds against a fielder taking a catch, but over the years this swagger mellowed into a geniality which made him among the most loved of men. Barry Jarman, whom he displaced in the Australian side, said, 'He was one of the game's greatest characters. I never begrudged playing second fiddle to him.'

Wally Grout had one game for Queensland in 1946–7 when Tallon was injured, but he had to wait another seven years before taking over permanently. Perhaps it was his reputation as a brash young man that made the Queensland selectors initially reject Grout as Tallon's deputy and choose Doug Siggs; whatever it was, he was twenty-six before he had the chance to play regularly for the state and advance his claims for a Test place.

Maddocks and Jarman kept him out at first, but he was selected as first-choice keeper for the tour to South Africa in 1957–8, and in the second innings of his first Test he established a Test record with six catches. This record was later equalled by Lindsay and John Murray, and beaten in 1979 by Wasim Bari.

Grout was to make five more overseas tours and play in four home series. In fifty-one Test matches he was to account for 187 batsmen, 163 of them caught and 24 stumped, and when his Test career ended, only Godfrey Evans could better that record.

He had 20 victims when Australia regained the Ashes in 1958–9 and 21 when they retained them in 1961, but his most memorable series was the one which preceded this. Australia and the West Indies began with the famous tied Test and ended with Australia winning the final Test by 2 wickets on the fifth afternoon. Grout had 20 catches and 3 stumpings in that exciting series. He had seven dismissals in the historic first Test, but three times in Test matches he was to account for eight batsmen.

He kept to a variety of bowlers: Benaud, McKenzie, Davidson, Mackay, Kline, Hawke, Lindwall, and the more doubtful actions of Meckiff and Rorke. He was the model of consistency and his own particular trademark was his spectacular diving catches – which thrilled the crowd – on the leg-side when standing back to the fast bowlers.

He advanced the fashion of standing back to the medium-pace bowlers and, as Brian Johnston remembers, he certainly caused some raised eyebrows by standing back to the slow-medium seam bowling of 'Slasher' Mackay. It was his style, capitalizing on his wonderful agility, and he missed very, very little. He was one upon whom the bowlers could rely.

He crouched low, ready to spring at the deflection, and, invariably, there was no leg-slip, so that he covered that area with his bounding agility. Bobby Simpson, at first slip, would stand wide so that Grout was given room to dive on the off, and the theory was that, whatever the liabilities of standing back, he gave an extra dimension to the catching arc behind the wicket.

His record speaks for itself. Bobby Simpson said simply, 'He was the greatest wicket-keeper I ever saw.' This was a sentiment echoed by Wes Hall, the magnificent West Indian fast bowler who played for Queensland with Grout. Grout's association with Alan Davidson at Test level accounted for 45 batsmen, one of the leading combinations between bowler and wicket-keeper at Test level.

In February 1960 he held eight catches in Western Australia's first innings against Queensland. It is a feat that has never been equalled in first-class cricket, although Derek Taylor of Somerset, one of the most consistent and best of keepers in county cricket in the late

1970s and early 1980s, took eight catches in the Benson & Hedges Cup match between Somerset and Combined Universities at Taunton on 8 May 1982. This success won him the Gold Award, quite an achievement for a wicket-keeper, whose skills so often go unrecognized in these matches.

Wally Grout was esteemed by all who played with and against him, and an incident in the first Test at Trent Bridge in 1964, his last tour to England, showed why he was so universally popular.

This was Boycott's first Test match and at practice on the morning of the match, John Edrich, who was to have been Boycott's opening partner, twisted an ankle and was unfit to play. Fred Titmus substituted as opener and stayed with Boycott for an hour while 36 were scored. During the course of their stand, Boycott pushed a ball to Neil Hawke at mid-on and the batsmen dashed for a quick single. Hawke dived for the ball and, in doing so, collided with Titmus and brought him down. The ball was returned to Grout with Titmus far from home, but he declined to break the wicket and allowed Titmus to make his ground. It was an act that was typical of this unfailingly cheerful man.

It was not known until later that, following the tour of England and shortly before the Australians set out for the West Indies, Grout suffered a heart attack. He was told by a Brisbane doctor that it was unwise for him to make the trip and that, in fact, he was endangering his health by playing at all. He was warned that he could collapse at any time, but he loved the game and balanced the joy it gave him, and the joy he gave to others, against extending his life by a few more years if he left it. His sense of fun never deserted him and his team-mates had no idea whatsoever as to his condition.

He made the tour of the West Indies, making 18 dismissals in the series, and then kept in all five Tests against Mike Smith's team in 1965–6. He retired at the end of the series, having taken four catches in the first innings of his last Test match. It was not simply the number of his dismissals or his exciting diving catches that marked his great skill, but his ability to encourage and lift his team-mates with his unflagging zest for the game.

At the beginning of November 1968 he suffered a serious heart attack and died in a Brisbane hospital a few days later. The world of cricket mourned him deeply. A light had gone out of many people's lives.

The family love of cricket was maintained by his daughter, who became a respected umpire in men's matches in Queensland.

13

The Golden Age of
Godfrey Evans

Sir,

I'll tell Tony Lewis why it is better for the wicket-keeper to stand up to the medium-pacers. It helps the fielding side to keep on top of the batsman and it helps the fielding side to keep on top of its job.

Psychologically, I am certain that the batsman feels more restricted if the wicket-keeper is standing up. He knows he cannot take guard outside the crease. He cannot go for a walk, and he knows he must always be thinking about the position of his feet, otherwise he might get stumped.

I also doubt whether the wicket-keeper standing back *does* hold more catches. He misses plenty that don't carry to him and these compensate for the difficult ones he might miss if he is standing up. He never stumps anybody, either.

Not only that, I am certain that if the wicket-keeper is standing up, the whole effort of the fielding side gets a lift. They have got someone to throw at. They know where he is, they can relate their position to him at all times and their work is nothing like as sloppy as it is when the wicket-keeper is running backwards and forwards all the time.

I always wore ordinary gloves and my hands are unmarked, except for my little fingers. I broke those in diving for low catches and stubbing my hands into the ground, *not* through taking the ball.

The author of this letter to *The Cricketer*, written seven years after he had retired from the game, was Godfrey Evans. 'He was,' as 'Hopper' Levett describes him, 'the last of the old great ones.'

The philosophy of wicket-keeping that Evans expounds in his letter is no idle ruminating from a man in his middle-forties dreaming of past glories. It is a statement of what he practised, for, in an age when other wicket-keepers were turning into long-stops, Godfrey Evans, by his own vital example, showed them to be the 'pedestrian practitioners that they were'.

Evans had balance, bounce, devilry, impishness and 'a flair for menacing the batsman with the slick snap of his intaking gloves and the whip of his wrists over the bails'. It is doubtful whether, in the whole history of the game, there has been a wicket-keeper more loved by those who paid to watch him.

He first played for England against Australia when Tallon was the opposing keeper; when he last played against Australia Grout was the opposing stumper. He appeared in his ninety-first and last Test, against India, later the same year in June 1959, and when he stumped Gupte off Greenough it was his 219th victim in Test cricket.

It was a remarkable achievement for one who, if the last of the great wicket-keepers, was unquestionably the most unorthodox of them. He violated the accepted principle of wicket-keeping by placing his weight forward on his toes. The other great wicket-keepers had all been quiet and unobtrusive; Evans was never quiet for a moment. He bubbled incessantly, darting one way and flinging himself another to bring off catches that were not even recognized as possible by others. No wicket-keeper has ever given greater joy; none has appeared to have had more joy in the game.

It was predicted that his style, a rejection of the flat-footed stance that would have given him more balance, was too dependent on his wonderful physical gifts of vitality and activity to see his career last very long; but he played Test cricket for thirteen years, and it was only when he saw the first signs of his dominance in the field waning that he retired from the game to which he had given so much.

Educated at Kent College, where his love of cricket was nurtured, Evans was taken on the Kent staff at the age of sixteen as a hard-hitting batsman who could also keep wicket, although his experience in this field was limited. It was Jack Durston and Harry Sharp who advised him to concentrate on improving his wicket-keeping because, having seen him at an indoor cricket school, they did not feel that he could curb his natural attacking tendencies enough to become a first-class batsman.

A chunky, solid individual, Evans also had an interest in boxing and he obtained a professional licence in 1937. He had three professional fights as a welterweight, winning the first two by a knock-out and the third on points. Unfortunately, in the third bout he received a broken nose. The contest had been on the eve of the cricket season and when he reported to Kent he was told that he would have to make a choice between boxing and cricket. He chose cricket.

He is adamant that his brief boxing career improved his cricket, and especially his wicket-keeping, as it developed his speed of footwork: 'It enabled me to take those very wide balls with a quick sway and without losing balance, and gave me greater reach than I might have had. I gave a lot of thought to my footwork.'

He received much help from Les Ames and 'Hopper' Levett in his early days with Kent, and it was Ames's back injury that gave him the chance to play in the first XI, although in his debut match against Surrey at Blackheath in 1939 he was chosen solely as batsman in order to give him a taste of county cricket.

He was retained for the next match, against Derbyshire at Gravesend, and kept wicket for the first time in a first-class game. He never forgets that 'Hopper' Levett, in wishing him luck, told him not to worry about missed chances and byes. He feels that it was the best advice he was ever given and it sustained him throughout his career.

Trevor Bailey maintained that it was his ability to put misses behind him that was one of Evans's greatest assets, and he quotes an incident when Evans dropped Neil Harvey off his bowling in a Test at Old Trafford: 'Neil had just come to the crease, and managed to get an outside edge. It travelled sweetly to Godfrey, standing back, who was throwing it and appealing when down it went. Throughout Neil's hundred I was haunted by that moment, but not Godfrey.'

Evans's first catch in first-class cricket occurred very early in the Derbyshire innings. The second ball of the second over of the innings, bowled by Norman Harding, took the inside edge of R. H. R. Buckston's bat and flew down the leg-side. Evans took off, stuck out his left hand and caught the ball as he landed. It was a spectacular catch that was to set a pattern for the years to come.

He was in and out of the Kent side for the remainder of the season, sometimes keeping wicket, sometimes being played for his batting. He gained a mention in *Wisden* after the match against Lancashire at Dover: 'Evans, seventeen years of age, kept wicket specially well on the first day.' *Wisden* was, in fact, mistaken. The match was played a week after his nineteenth birthday. It was also a week before the outbreak of the Second World War.

He joined the Royal Army Service Corps in the summer of 1940. He became a sergeant and it was while playing for the army in some of those magnificent matches that adorned Lord's in the dark days of the war that he came into prominence. He played for England in a memorable two-day match against the Dominions and was asked to play in the Victory Tests, but he was unable to do so as he was posted to Germany.

On the resumption of first-class cricket after the war, with Les Ames having given up wicket-keeping and Levett now thirty-seven, Evans became Kent's first-choice stumper. He was not selected for the Test trial when S. C. Griffith of Sussex and Haydn Davies of Glamorgan, a neat, reliable keeper of outstanding ability who never gained his just reward, were chosen, nor for the first two Tests against India when Paul Gibb was the keeper. He was, however, selected for the second Test trial at Canterbury, the third Test against India, and to tour Australia with Wally Hammond's team in 1946–7.

Paul Gibb was the first-choice keeper for that tour and played in the first Test, but war had deprived him of more than most and he faded from the scene. Evans played against Australia for the first time at Sydney in

December 1946. Australia scored 659. Evans caught Miller off Peter Smith and did not concede a bye. In the third Test, at Melbourne, Australia scored 365 in their first innings. Evans caught Miller and Tallon and did not concede a bye. It was a remarkable record in Test cricket – 1024 runs without conceding a bye.

In the second innings of that Melbourne Test he caught McCool off Alec Bedser, the first time that the two had combined in a Test match to dismiss a batsman. Bedser consistently paid tribute to Evans's wicket-keeping and what it did for him as a bowler. The keeper was always up close to the stumps and would bound with the ball that lifted sharply on the leg-side. There was a unity between this bowler and keeper which few other combinations have ever achieved and it cannot be measured simply by the number of victims that they shared.

Trevor Bailey remembers a festival match at Scarborough when Billy Sutcliffe glanced a delivery from Bedser wide off the full face of the bat. Evans, anticipating, took off and caught the ball one-handed while horizontal. But even when he was not pulling off sensational catches or lightning stumpings, he was always a threat off Bedser's bowling.

He showed another facet of his character in the fourth Test match at Adelaide. England trailed by 27 in the first innings and were 255 for 8 in their second when Evans joined Denis Compton, who was 43 not out. England, with only Doug Wright to come, faced defeat.

Evans batted for 95 minutes before he scored a run and, in all, batted for 2½ hours for 10 not out, facing ninety-eight deliveries and scoring off only seven of them. Compton scored a century and the match was saved.

In one respect the innings was quite untypical of Godfrey Evans. He was a hitter, always looking for a chance to score, but, above all, he was a fighter and he relished the scrap and the occasion of this stand with Compton. In contrast, in the Lord's Test against India in 1952 he hit 104 out of 159 in 2 hours 10 minutes. At lunch he was 98 not out. The batsman he overshadowed was Tom Graveney.

Evans was a very good batsman who could never quite be persuaded to take his batting as seriously as he should have done. He hit seven centuries in his career and two of them were in Test matches. Perhaps this is a pointer to what his critics insist, that he was a better player at Test level than he was at county level. Certainly, he did not perform consistently well behind the stumps for Kent, but this was not because of a lack of mental strength, as some have suggested, but because he thrived on the big occasion, on the large audience. They lifted him, as the occasion lifted him, and he lifted them in return.

His style was extrovert and joyful, and so his bad days, like those of an actor, were clearly discernible. At Leeds in 1948, when England had a chance of beating Australia for the first time since 1938, he missed stumping both Morris and Bradman as Australia scored 404 for 3 to win on the last day. He had a nightmare match, but Bill O'Reilly could still write of him at the end of the tour: 'He is by far the most energetic keeper I have ever seen. He seems prepared not only to do his own particular job of work but also to relieve the in-fieldsmen of some of theirs. His leg-side keeping has reached a standard seldom attained by any other modern keeper.'

An example of what O'Reilly meant about Evans relieving some of the in-fieldsmen of their duties was to be seen in the Test trial at Bradford in 1950. Jim Laker took 8 for 2 as the Rest of England were spun out for 27. In their second innings they succumbed to Hollies and Laker for 113. Evans's keeping on a brutal, sticky wicket could not have been bettered. One of Laker's first innings victims was Don Kenyon, who moved back to a ball that turned and lifted violently. Kenyon, who was top scorer with 7, played the ball down, but Evans dived forwards to catch the ball one-handed in front of the batsman. None of the cluster of short-legs had moved.

Trevor Bailey said firmly, 'Godfrey Evans was, quite simply, the finest wicket-keeper I have seen. At his very best he was capable of making catches and stumpings which no other man would have considered chances.'

As already mentioned he accepted advice from Ames,

Levett, and, in Australia, from Oldfield, who recommended that he link his little fingers to keep his hands
moving in unison. Nevertheless, having absorbed and
welcomed advice, his style and method were his own. He
jettisoned wicket-keepers' pads in favour of batsmen's
pads in order to gain more mobility, and he wanted gloves
that were soft and pliable so that he could 'feel' the ball.

Evans was reared in a Kent second XI side that had
Gerard Simpson as its captain. Simpson led the side until
1949, when he was sixty-three. He was no great tactician,
but he had a great conviction that cricket was a game of
fun, something to be enjoyed. If that was a lesson Evans
ever needed teaching, he certainly learned it well.

Those years just after the Second World War were a
time when people yearned for fun. They had survived a
terrible war and were living through a period of austerity
as the country struggled to rebuild. They had been
starved of entertainment and colour, and in characters
like Compton, Edrich and Evans they found a release for
the reservoirs of joy that had been stored.

Evans loved life and he laughed his way through it,
taking the spectators with him. If cricket were in danger
of becoming dull or pedestrian, it needed only an infusion
of Godfrey Evans's spirits to revitalize it. In an age when
drabness and lack of personality had threatened to domi-
nate, he infected people with his inexhaustible vitality and
optimism. Never flippant in his approach to the game, he
inspired bowlers to greater efforts by his buoyancy. As
Fingleton said of him, 'Nothing is impossible for Evans
behind the stumps.'

It should not be thought that Evans's keeping was
merely intuitive. He thought deeply about the subject,
analysed what he was doing, discussed with other players,
and wrote and lectured on the art. He set down five
simple, basic principles of wicket-keeping to which he
adhered.

First, he insisted on a good view of the ball. He would
mark a line behind the off-stump with his boot and place
his left foot on that line and his right foot a comfortable
distance from it. This gave him his sense of position and

a clear view so that he could move in either direction quickly. Second, he insisted on balance, but, as previously noted, his method of achieving balance was not consistent with what others had practised. Concentration was his third principle and, like most other keepers, he considered lapses in concentration to be the chief causes of failure, and unflagging concentration to be the most difficult thing to achieve. He emphasized, as his fourth principle, that it was essential that the hands should give with the ball and never snatch; and, lastly, he felt it was necessary, wherever practicable, to get the body behind the ball.

Like all good precepts, these rules seem deceptively naïve when set down, and Evans made no claim to any profundity in them; but if any keeper could maintain them consistently, he would be a good keeper. They do not, however, explain Evans's greatness. What was the secret of this? Trevor Bailey answers the question:

Apart from sheer ability and a superb eye, it was very largely a matter of vitality. Many people can be brilliant for a short period of time, but it takes a very exceptional person to be just as full of life and just as spectacular an hour before the close of play on a really hot day at Adelaide after five successive sessions in the field. The fact that Godfrey Evans was a born entertainer who welcomed the limelight, and possessed a flair for the spectacular and the audacious, not only made him a universal favourite with spectators; it acted also as a spur to the fielders to maintain the standard he set himself.

In two respects Godfrey was fortunate. He was able to take a swift nap and awake refreshed under the most difficult circumstances. On numerous occasions I have seen him come in at lunchtime, have a drink and then curl up and go to sleep, completely oblivious to the noise of the dressing room. The other reason underlying his success was his ability to dismiss instantly from his mind any mistake he might make.

A temporary loss of form cost Evans his Test place in the last two matches against South Africa in 1948–9, 'Billy' Griffith replacing him, but for over a decade he was an automatic selection. No other wicket-keeper came within a mile of him. In the opinion of most people, he was still

streets ahead of all opposition in 1958–9, but the selectors
began to include Swetman upon occasions.

Evans played in the first two Tests in the 1959 series
against India, which England won easily. Swetman was
chosen for the third Test, Evans being omitted, the selectors announced, 'in the interests of team building'. Realizing that the selectors were trying to find his successor and
that his supremacy was waning, he retired from the game
at the end of the 1959 season.

It was not quite the end for Evans. In 1967 Kent
had their best season for thirty-nine years. They won the
Gillette Cup and finished as runners-up to Yorkshire in
the County Championship. They were neck-and-neck
with Yorkshire when the teams met at Canterbury in
August. Knott and Underwood were away on Test duty
and Kent brought Evans out of retirement a week before
his forty-seventh birthday to keep wicket in the vital
match. He kept superbly, catching Taylor and Illingworth, and the large crowds attending the match loved
him. He was now more portly, with bushy whiskers down
the side of his face, but he was as dapper as ever and
doing the thing he loved most in all the world.

He suffered much when he first left cricket. His vitality
has never diminished, but he lost direction. Now he is an
integral part of the cricket world again. He lays the odds
for Ladbrooke's at all the big matches and he assists
Gilbey's in their wicket-keeping awards, a most valuable
and praiseworthy addition to the game.

He can be seen on many grounds, red-faced and chirpy,
like Mr Jorrocks out for a stroll, secure in the knowledge
that the hunt and the saddle of mutton await him at
home. Frequently, people whom he has never met will
wave to him and say, 'Hello, Godfrey.' And he will smile
and wave back cheerily. Like Arnold Bennett's character,
he is one of those people who was sent on earth to make
the rest of us happy.

14

Murray and Parks:
the Great Debate

The end of the reign of a hero who has become part of folklore is not an easy thing to accept, and even at the distance of twenty-five years, it is impossible to understand how captain Peter May and his selectors could have conceived of Roy Swetman as an adequate replacement for Godfrey Evans.

When England had toured Australia in 1954–5, the famous series in which Hutton's side, with Tyson as the spearhead, had retained the Ashes, Keith Andrew of Northamptonshire had been reserve to Evans. Andrew played in the first Test because Evans had sunstroke. His next and last Test was to be nine years later. In his first Test Andrew had the misfortune to drop Arthur Morris off Alec Bedser before he had scored, and Morris went on to score 153.

Andrew was a quiet and efficient wicket-keeper who was the inspiration to Bob Taylor and, indeed, to many others. In his early days as a keeper, Eifion Jones remembers seeing Andrew keep wicket to the medium pace of Crump on a spiteful pitch at Cardiff. 'It was unbelievable,' he says. 'I have never seen an exhibition to compare with it. It would have taught any budding keeper all he needed to know about concentrating on the line of the ball.'

Perhaps Andrew was so unobtrusive in his wicket-keeping that he was taken for granted. He kept for and captained his county with distinction, but in an age when wicket-keepers were being pushed back by the obsession for pace, he was a better player standing up than standing back where he lacked the agility of some of his rivals. He served on the Northants committee and later on the Lancashire committee, and he is now a most respected chief coach of the National Cricket Association.

Andrew went to the West Indies with Peter May's team in 1959–60. He suffered a virus infection early in the tour and he had a somewhat shaky start, after which he performed splendidly, but it was Swetman who kept in the first four Tests.

Peter May was taken ill on the tour and returned home. His replacement was Jim Parks, who had been coaching in Trinidad. Swetman's wicket-keeping and batting declined on the tour and it was obvious that he was not up to Test standard. Of Andrew, *Wisden* wrote: '. . . because of the desire to include a wicket-keeper-batsman he received few chances. In fact, he took part in only four first-class matches and played but one innings as a batsman. He must have felt somewhat frustrated at the small amount of cricket which came his way.'

The inclusion of Parks in the final Test and 'the desire to include a wicket-keeper-batsman' was to begin a controversy which has lasted until this day. It was the birth of the slighting of the wicket-keeper's art.

Jim Parks is a man of great charm. In the early 1950s he was one of the most exciting young batsmen in England. Quick on his feet, he attacked the spinners with great panache and was a delight to watch. He fielded brilliantly in the covers and his cricket was a joy. In 1954 he was picked to play for England against Pakistan in the third Test at Old Trafford. He scored 15 and was selected neither for the fourth Test, nor for the tour of Australia for which Colin Cowdrey was the surprise choice. It was generally felt that Parks had been done a great injustice, but that his exciting batting would win him a place in the England side before long.

He enjoyed a very good season in 1956 and was selected for the MCC team to South Africa, but he was taken ill after one match and returned home to England. The reserve wicket-keeper on that tour was Brian Taylor, who was to rejuvenate Essex a decade later. Two young keepers had been in line for the job of Evans's understudy, and most people had been surprised that it was Taylor and not John Murray of Middlesex who had got the selection.

In 1958 Robin Marlar, the Sussex captain, asked Jim Parks if he would try his luck behind the stumps; the thought behind the suggestion was that one of the amateur batsmen could then be included during the holidays. Parks had operated as an emergency wicket-keeper because he was so good a fielder, but his first experience proper behind the stumps was in the match against Yorkshire at Worthing at the end of July. He took one catch, but it was not a particularly auspicious debut. In his own words, Parks found the job very difficult:

A batsman has to concentrate all the time he is at the wicket receiving a ball, but he does have a respite when the other batsman is on guard. But not a wicket-keeper. He has to concentrate upon every ball bowled during the innings, and it did not take me long to understand I did not possess the necessary concentration. This power of concentration can only be developed after considerable experience behind the stumps. It makes a newcomer mentally tired, while the physical demands are far greater than I ever imagined.

It was believed that Jim Parks would only keep the wicket-keeping job until the end of the season because the regular stumper, Rupert Webb, was injured. However, Robin Marlar suggested that he should remain in the position in 1959, a suggestion which did not please Parks at first. He had a marvellous summer, scoring 2313 runs and taking 93 dismissals, 86 caught and 7 stumped. He was still quick to state that he considered himself a batsman first and a wicket-keeper second, and that if he found the keeping interfering with his batting, he would surrender the job.

The changing pattern of wicket-keeping could already be seen in that Parks's 93 dismissals contained only 7 stumpings. When Hugo Yarnold, a dapper, competent and quick keeper, had dismissed 110 batsmen in 1949, 47 of them had been stumpings. Yarnold's successor in the

Worcestershire side, Roy Booth, had 89 victims in 1959, 101 in 1960 and 100 in 1964, and of those only 6, 16 and 9, respectively, were stumped. In three seasons, he could accomplish only two thirds of the number of stumpings that Yarnold had managed in 1949, but he was no lesser a wicket-keeper.

Parks arrived on the scene as pace dominated. There was still the legacy of Ames: if a great batsman could also be a great wicket-keeper, why should not others follow suit? But, as John Murray says, 'Les was in a class of his own. There's never been anybody else to touch him.' And John Murray is the only other wicket-keeper ever to have scored 1000 runs and dismissed 100 batsmen in a season.

In 1959–60 Trueman and Statham were England's leading wicket-takers in the Tests, and Ramadhin, Hall and Watson led for the West Indies. Alexander had 23 dismissals as he captained the West Indies from behind the stumps, and 22 of them were catches. The three England spinners, Allen, Illingworth and Barrington, could not muster as many wickets between them in the Tests as Trueman took, and they were appreciably more expensive, but the spinner as an attacking bowler was beginning to disappear and containment was the key word.

Paradoxically, two of Parks's first three victims in Test cricket, Walcott and Hunte, were stumped. He had joined the side just before the fifth and final Test and scored 183 at Berbice. He was preferred to Swetman in the final Test and scored 43 and 101 not out in a drawn match. In fact, he was to play another forty-four Tests and score only one more century, but to have a batsman of his class coming in at number seven or number eight was certainly an advantage.

He played in all five Tests against South Africa in 1960, but his form with the bat was poor and his wicket-keeping, still in an embryo state, was mediocre. It was now that the clamour for John Murray began to be heard more loudly.

Murray was a Londoner, warm and vital. A batsman of great natural elegance, he was accepted on to the Lord's ground staff at the age of fourteen, but the school-leaving age was raised and he had to stay on at school for another year. Most of his cricket, and soccer, was played for Rugby Boys' Club near his home in Notting Hill. He was playing in the final of the Boys' Club competition when the Club's wicket-keeper broke a finger. He recalls what followed:

I don't know why, but I volunteered to take over and kept for the rest of the match. I'd never kept wicket before. Our warden, Paul Pawson, said to me afterwards that I should stick to wicket-keeping as I could be good at it. He got on to Archie Fowler at Lord's and told him that when I turned up they should have a look at me as a wicket-keeper.

As soon as I arrived at Lord's they put me in the nets and told me to keep wicket. Within two years I was in the Middlesex first team.

They tried to make me an opening batsman as well, but I was never suited to that. I made a conscious decision to concentrate on my wicket-keeping and I never paid as much attention to my batting as I should have done. Perhaps I was wrong, but I loved the wicket-keeping and I had to work hard at it. People used to say to me later that I always made it look so easy, but I was working very hard inside myself.

I could get runs when we needed them, but at other times I got out too often to bad bowlers.

The only coaching I ever received in wicket-keeping was from Bert Strudwick and Andy Wilson. I was doing National Service in the RAF and Middlesex arranged for me to have two days' leave in the April and spend it with Gloucestershire as that was where I was stationed. I had two days chatting to Andy Wilson, who had been on the Lord's ground staff and was still very much a Middlesex man even though he was the Gloucestershire keeper.

The other piece of coaching came when Jim Sims, our scorer, asked Struddie, who was scoring for Surrey, to come in an hour early for the three days of the match when we were playing Surrey, and give me a few tips. He did. He talked to me mostly about leg-side work. That was the only formal training I had of any sort.

I was on the Arsenal's books as an amateur. I was an inside-forward, and when Tommy Lawton was manager of Brentford he asked me to turn pro, but I decided to stick to cricket. Les

Compton was getting on and I thought that there would be a regular place for me in the Middlesex side. I loved cricket more than football and I've no regrets. Football doesn't interest me now as it used to. I sometimes go with my son, and Alan Mullery and I have been friends for years and are cousins by marriage, but it doesn't have the appeal for me that it used to. I am very glad that I stuck to cricket.

John Murray left the RAF for a regular place in the Middlesex side in 1956. A year later he became only the second player in cricket history to achieve the wicket-keeper's double when he scored 1025 runs and claimed 104 victims, 82 caught and 22 stumped. His partnership with Fred Titmus had begun to flourish. In 1960 he reached the keeper's century for the second time when he caught 95 and stumped 7 in the season.

With such an impressive record, his claims could be denied no longer and he was chosen for his first Test match when England played Australia at Edgbaston in June 1961. He had toured New Zealand with the MCC 'A' team under Dennis Silk earlier in the year and had outshone Jim Parks. Now he had secured the Test place and finished the series with a record 18 dismissals. He gave five impeccable performances and was generally accepted as the natural heir to Godfrey Evans's kingdom.

He won acclaim as a stylist, superb in all that he did. Here was a purist of the old school.

With television now a dominant factor in international cricket reportage, Murray's style became known to millions. Immaculate in dress, he would go through a studied ritual with his white-backed gloves before settling on his haunches. The gloves would be touched together in front of his face and the hands would describe a graceful arc before he crouched:

I didn't know that I was doing it, but Denis Compton was commentating on the Tests and he had noticed it. He came to me at lunchtime in one of the Tests and said, 'I'm on at three o'clock and I'm going to draw people's attention to your mannerisms.' I didn't know what he was talking about and then everybody began to tell me.

The person I owed it to was Wally Grout. What a keeper! Do you remember the way he used to throw the ball back to the bowler? Everything he did had rhythm. I watched him and I thought that's what I want to be like, so I tried to imitate his smoothness and get rid of my coarse edges.

I could never have been like Godfrey. God knows how many catches and stumpings Godfrey missed. It didn't matter. He just threw the ball back and bounced on. But you can't copy people like Godfrey, they're unique.

The grace and elegance of Murray's wicket-keeping in that series established him as a man incapable of an ineloquent gesture, one whose every movement was aesthetically pleasing. Even when he tossed the ball to first slip it was an act of beauty.

He was an automatic choice for the tour of Pakistan and India in 1961–2 and all began well. He had three catches off three bowlers of different types among the first 4 wickets to fall in the first Test in Pakistan, but when the side moved on to India a fortnight later he had an unhappy first Test, conceding 33 byes in India's first innings. He seemed better in the second Test, but after the third it was revealed that he was suffering from varicose veins and he was flown home to England for an operation. Geoff Millman of Notts took over in the remaining Tests and Jimmy Binks was flown out as replacement.

Murray played a little too soon at the beginning of 1962, but, after a short rest, quickly regained form and won back his Test place from Millman. He kept with all his old panache and went to Australia with Ted Dexter's team, not only as England's number one wicket-keeper, but as the number one wicket-keeper in the world. There were, however, some disquieting rumours. Expressing the view that he was the best wicket-keeper in the world to county cricketers, one was met with agreement, but also with the suggestion that he wouldn't play in the Tests as Dexter didn't like him. It should be clarified immediately that there was no personal antagonism between the two men, but, as Ted Dexter has admitted since, he 'wasn't very good at wicket-keepers'. Dexter's feeling was that he had seen the specialist keepers, like Murray and Andrew, drop catches, so one might as well play a first-rate batsman who could put the gloves on and do an adequate, if not outstanding job.

'Hopper' Levett, with the wisdom of years, assesses: 'Internationally, there was nothing in John Murray's class. He was streets ahead of anyone else and he would have been a better keeper still if he had someone really pushing him, but there wasn't. That he didn't play more is a mystery, but it only needs one committee member to dislike you and you are done for.'

It was not that Murray was disliked, but the 1962–3 tour of Australia must rank among the most bizarre ever to have taken place.

The first strange events concerned the selection of the party. The Rev. David Sheppard, who had played very little first-class cricket since going into the ministry, was chosen and his earlier absence from the game was reflected in the number of catches that this once fine fielder missed in the early part of the tour. Naturally enough, he spent much of his time on the tour away from the team as guest preacher, so that he appeared to be more on an evangelical mission than on a trip to regain the Ashes.

The choice of the Duke of Norfolk as manager of the party also roused much comment. It remains a bewildering appointment to this day. A man with a great love of the game and respected by the players, he was, nevertheless, unable to carry out his duties as fully as was necessary, returning as he did to England for six weeks in the middle of the tour to fulfil his official functions.

Equally puzzling was the choice of A. C. Smith as reserve wicket-keeper to John Murray. Millman, Parks and Binks were all overlooked and a wicket-keeper of moderate accomplishment, without the bonus of being a batsman of Test class, was chosen. A likeable man of intelligence and good humour who has served the game nobly as an administrator since his retirement, A. C.

Smith was a dashing captain of Oxford University and later of Warwickshire, but he was never a player approaching Test standard.

It was apparent, however, from the start of the tour that there was a lobby in favour of Smith as first-choice wicket-keeper, and this became very obvious when Murray's chances in the first-class games became limited so that he played only twice to Smith's four times before the first Test. Smith played against New South Wales, in the next match against Queensland, and then in the first Test which followed. It is interesting to reflect what Australian opinion was, for a school named its four houses after members of the touring party – one house was called Murray.

After playing in the first two Tests, Smith was dropped. Murray came in for the game at Sydney. England made 279 and Australia had made 14 in reply when Lawry touched Coldwell down the leg-side. Murray was always a keeper of exceptional agility: as the ball flew down the leg-side from the intended glance, he dived to his right and took the ball one-handed, inches from the ground. Unfortunately, in doing so, he damaged his shoulder badly and after struggling on for a few more overs, was forced to leave the field. Parfitt kept wicket for the rest of the match, which England lost.

Murray received a wrong diagnosis and treatment, which delayed the healing process, but although he was fit for the fifth Test, Smith played and had a poor match. The team went on to New Zealand where Murray was told that he would play in the first Test and Smith in the second, and then they would see about the third. Smith scored 69 not out in the second Test and shared a ninth-wicket stand of 163 with Colin Cowdrey, and it was he who played in the third Test, which proved to be the end of his international career.

For the first Test against the West Indies in 1963 Keith Andrew was chosen as wicket-keeper. He gave a quietly effective performance but that was the end of his Test career. Jim Parks was recalled for the last four Tests.

This was the series in which Deryck Murray, appearing for the first time, had 24 victims. He was to become the only West Indian keeper to pass 100 dismissals in Test cricket.

Parks was now considered first-choice wicket-keeper and Jimmy Binks went as his reserve on the tour of India under Mike Smith in 1963–4. The team was depleted by injuries and illness, and both men played in the second and third Tests, with Binks keeping wicket.

Binks, a late-order batsman for Yorkshire, opened in three of his four Test innings, scoring 55 at Brabourne Stadium, Bombay. At Calcutta he took five catches in the first innings and his Test career was then over.

He was a polished and dedicated professional, superbly competent in all that he did, although probably at his best when standing up, even to the brisk medium of Nicholson and Appleyard. His outstanding season was 1960 when he caught 97 and stumped 11, a total number of catches which has not been surpassed. He was a strong keeper and played 412 consecutive County Championship matches for Yorkshire. Yorkshiremen still feel aggrieved, with total justification, that he played in only two Test matches, and then only because batsmen and bowlers were unavailable.

Parks now had an uninterrupted run as England's keeper. In all, he played forty-six Test matches, scored nearly 2000 Test runs and dismissed 114 batsmen in Test cricket. He was safe and efficient, if not dramatic, when standing back, and adequate when standing up. The sad thing was that, in taking over the wicket-keeping role, his batting never sustained the brilliant heights of which it was capable. He had the promise and excitement of a Denis Compton, which were frittered away because he gave so much energy to a job for which he was only partly suited.

Did John Murray ever get upset or bitter about not being chosen as England's keeper when the majority of people believed that he was better than any other in the world?

Of course, I can't pretend I didn't at times, but we were all good friends. Jim and I got on very well, and you have to take these things or you won't last very long in the game.

I got upset once in South Africa. I was batting well and keeping well, but Jim played in the first Test and got a hundred. I got some runs in the match after that and then I was given some time off with a couple of the other lads so that we could have a special trip over the Kruger National Park. We were about an hour outside Pretoria and we stopped for coffee or something and there was a message that Jim was unwell and couldn't play and I'd have to go back to Pretoria. I rushed back and played. I kept well and when I went in we were 134 for 6. I scored 142 and we passed 300 and won.

I felt good and Mike Smith came up to me just before the second Test and said, 'Sorry, J.T., you're not in.' I said something rude to him because I was very disappointed, but he was great at handling people and an hour later he came back with a gin and tonic for me and we sat and laughed.

Towards the end of that tour England decided that Murray could solve the opening batsman/slip catching problem that existed, and he played in the fifth Test in those capacities. There are strange ways in cricket.

Parks retained his place in the England side the following summer and on the tour to Australia in 1965–6 when Murray was his deputy, but his batting was waning in power – a sad waste.

When Sobers brought the West Indian side to England in 1966 they swept all before them. Parks scored 91 in the second Test at Lord's, which was the only one of the first four Tests in which England avoided defeat.

For the last Test at the Oval, the England selectors made six changes. Brian Close replaced Colin Cowdrey as captain and John Murray was named as wicket-keeper in a side which had been completely restructured.

Facing a West Indian total of 268, England were 166 for 7 when Murray joined Tom Graveney. He just touched on to his pad the first ball he received, from Charlie Griffith, so escaping being l.b.w. Thereafter he played magnificently and shared a stand of 217. In 4½ hours he hit thirteen 4s and scored 112. England went on to win a memorable Test.

At his best Murray was a batsman of the very highest class and a particularly fine driver of the ball. Frank Worrell had said of him: 'If he didn't keep wicket, he would score over two thousand runs a season.' Perhaps the most important factor, however, as *Wisden* pointed out, was that his neat and efficient wicket-keeping did so much to raise the England fielding to Test standard, a standard which it had not attained for some time.

He was chosen for the series of three Tests against India the following season, and kept wicket rather indifferently at Headingley. In the first innings of the second Test at Lord's he missed a catch and asked umpire Syd Buller what he was doing wrong. Umpires are always a help, particularly if they have been keepers themselves. Eifion Jones, David East and others all say how much they owe to the observation of Barry Meyer, who will tell them that they are getting up too soon and should stay down until the ball pitches. This, in fact, was the advice that Buller gave Murray.

He quickly re-adjusted, found his rhythm again, and held six catches in the innings to equal the Test record held by Grout and Lindsay. It was his final Test triumph. He did not keep well at Edgbaston, nor in the first Test against Pakistan at Lord's, where he was out for a 'pair'. For the last two Tests against Pakistan, England chose a young man named Alan Knott.

Incomprehensibly, the selectors reverted to Parks as first choice for the tour of the West Indies, but Knott, his deputy, displaced him after the third Test and 'greatly raised the standard of wicket-keeping, which was otherwise unusually low in the series'.

Murray was back as Knott's understudy for the riot-ridden tour of Pakistan a year later, but he never played another Test match. He continued to enjoy the game, however, and the beauty of his wicket-keeping remained a fascination. He remembers how he felt:

The last five years were hard. You are living on experience then. Even great keepers like Knotty and Bob Taylor fall back on experience today. They don't go for things now that they would have gone for a few years ago. I had begun working for Derrick Robins, but he told me to keep playing so long as I wanted. I was still enjoying it because Fred was playing and I loved keeping to him more than to anyone else. He had so many variations. It kept you on your toes. It was always interesting.

I remember once, in the mid-sixties, we were playing Glamorgan, and Fred used to bowl a quicker one down the leg-side when he saw someone coming up the wicket to him. We'd worked this out beforehand because the idea was that we should try and work a stumping. In the second innings Rees kept going down the wicket so Fred gave me the nod. He bowled a wider, quicker one down the leg-side and Rees was stranded, so he dived and caught the ball. We appealed for handled ball and he had to go. He roared with laughter and we all stood there laughing. It was always good fun when Fred was bowling.

J.T. retired in 1975 when he was forty. His last season was a glory. He surpassed Herbert Strudwick's world record of 1493 dismissals and lifted it to 1527, of which 1270 were catches, another record. Mike Brearley wrote an appreciation of him in *Wisden* after 'twenty summers of almost infallible wicket-keeping and classic batsmanship'. Later in the year he was awarded the MBE.

His final game for Middlesex was in the Gillette Cup Final against Lancashire. He was cheered to the wicket. He scored 13, and when Lancashire batted he took a brilliant one-handed catch to dismiss Frank Hayes. But Middlesex lost, and they had been beaten in the Benson & Hedges Final earlier in the year; in Murray's time with them they had not won a trophy.

Derrick Robins, for whose teams Murray did so much, sold his business, and Murray worked for Slazenger's. A few years ago he went into his own business with his cousin, and Rodway Security Company, a firm which arranges security guards and facilities for various companies, was the outcome. He interviews and selects staff with the care, compassion and sensitivity that marked the warmth of his cricket.

He has remained very close to the game. He was a Test selector, but he resigned over the choice of Roger Tolchard for the 1978–9 tour to Australia. Tolchard was selected as a batsman who kept wicket, and Murray felt that this was neglecting his advice and disparaging the claims of some fine players. He finds it hard to understand, too, why a batsman is considered to need a fortnight or three weeks to acclimatize to a country whereas a wicket-keeper must expect to be flown out overnight and play in a Test match the next day if required. He remains a strong, purposeful man, whose common sense and integrity are still very much needed in the cricket world.

He is unquenchably a Middlesex man, and when he says, 'Our lad is very good', one knows he is referring to Paul Downton.

> A thing of beauty is a joy for ever:
> Its loveliness increases; it will never
> Pass into nothingness. . . .

John Murray's wicket-keeping was a thing of beauty, and when one closes one's eyes on a warm day at Lord's one can still see the touch of the cap as the gloved hands meet in front of the face, the gentle curve as he settles into position, and the liquid movement as the ball is taken and tossed to first slip.

15

Alan Knott:
a Fine Example

'And in all those Tests,' asks John Murray, 'how many batsmen did Godfrey Evans stump off Alec Bedser? Three? Two?'

It is the argument for standing back to the medium-pace bowler, and it is one which Alan Knott, in the opinion of many the finest wicket-keeper seen since the Second World War, echoes:

When I first played for Kent, Alan Dixon was usually one of the opening bowlers, and he liked the keeper standing up for his medium-paced swingers. Kent had had many years of keepers standing up to such bowlers and, being young and inexperienced, I followed tradition. For three seasons I stood up to Alan, and in all that time I remember only three stumpings off him, and two of those could hardly be ranked as genuine.

The first was at Leicester when Peter Marner allowed a wide delivery to go down the leg-side and, on watching me take the ball, unconsciously lifted his foot long enough for me to remove the bails. The other was at Canterbury against Somerset. Geoff 'Chimp' Clayton, that superbly safe Somerset and ex-Lancashire wicket-keeper, was batting with his ribs heavily strapped after injury. Alan again bowled a wide one down the leg-side and Geoff, restricted and in pain as he was, practically fell out of his ground when he tried to follow the line of the ball.

As the years passed I came to realize that there was little point in standing up to Alan if there were no stumping chances coming, so back I went to a position where I could take the thick-edged catches I would have had little or no chance of holding close to the stumps. Any catches, other than those edged fine, especially down the leg-side, can be difficult standing up, whereas standing back you will have far more chance of taking them comfortably.

It is a modern philosophy, the practicality of which has become apparent and one which has been fostered by the limited-over game.

Knott has gone as far as to say that the tradition of standing up to anyone who was a fraction slower than genuinely fast was a stupid example of pride and that wicket-keepers suffered dreadful and unnecessary finger injuries as a result, with no great quota of dismissals to show in return. Throughout his career he has been a positive thinker on the art of wicket-keeping, and no man has been more greatly admired and respected by his colleagues.

He followed the great Kent tradition almost by the same accident that marked the beginning of the wicket-keeping careers of Ames and Evans. His father was a wicket-keeper who played for Belvedere. Alan would join his father in practice and would dive and leap for catches which his father would provide when trying to bat with a stick; but Alan's early ambitions were to be a quick bowler, not a wicket-keeper.

His size, however, argued against pace and, under the tutelage of Claude Lewis, he turned to spin. He was asked to keep wicket in a couple of games for Kent Club and Ground, but when he joined the staff and played for the second XI it was as a spinner. Derek Ufton was second-team skipper and keeper, and Tony Catt held the first-team spot.

At the beginning of the 1964 season Ufton became manager of Plymouth Argyle FC and so severed his connection with Kent. Knott was now second-team wicket-keeper and at the end of June he made his first-team debut against Cambridge University, captained by Mike Brearley, at Folkestone. He took three catches and made the winning hit.

By the end of the season he had displaced Catt in the side, and in 1965 he was the first-choice keeper. Two years later he played his first match for England, against

Pakistan at Trent Bridge. He was twenty-one years old and he held seven catches, all of them different. At the Oval he had five catches and a stumping. It was a mighty beginning to a career which has seen him play in ninety-five Tests and account for 269 batsmen, an English record.

Knott's capabilities as a wicket-keeper were easily recognizable. Like Evans, he takes his stance with the weight on his toes. He shares Evans's vitality and activity, but Knott's is more nervous and less extrovert. Also, like Evans, he shows a real sense of enjoyment in the game, but once again it is marked by an introspection.

He has an eagerness behind the stumps which is a constant menace to the batsman. Dark-eyed, agile, small, he is an impish genius with powers of concentration as great as any in the game. This concentration is wedded to a dazzling speed of movement which allows him to dive to pick up the half-chance with the dexterity of a leopard leaping on its prey. His ability when standing up is no less brilliant, and his partnership with Derek Underwood for Kent and England has become legendary. He works close to the stumps and his neatness and quickness bring an economy to his style which explodes in triumph as the sharp edge or the lifted heel offers a chance.

His standard has been so consistently high that an error makes headline news. The most often heard criticism is of his tendency to stand back to medium-pace bowling, but his reasons for this policy have already been noted. Brian Johnston recalls how Knott approached him to write an article for his benefit brochure in 1976; Johnston agreed, but said that he would want paying. Knott looked somewhat aggrieved at this as it is not customary for contributors to ask for payment for articles in benefit brochures, but he asked Johnston what fee he wanted. 'I want to see you stand up to Bob Woolmer,' Johnston said. 'That's my fee.' Alan Knott smiled.

Throughout the season Knott stood back to Woolmer as was his custom, and then, in the fifth Test, when Woolmer was brought on to bowl, Knott looked up at the commentary box and took up a position behind the stumps for a couple of overs.

His adherence to the principle of standing back has been as strict as his adherence to his other principles, for he is a fastidious man who makes decisions after balanced thought. On the advice of Keith Andrew, whom he greatly admires, he warms his hands in near-boiling water before going on the field, and he has always worn his shirt collar up as a shield against sunstroke and his shirt sleeves down as a protection for his arms when he dives. A handkerchief is always protruding from his pocket, seemingly the same amount visible at all times as if accurately measured.

The capped figure is immediately recognizable on any ground. In profile, he is akin to Mr Punch. His rapidity of movement does nothing to distort the comparison. Yet he is not a naturally supple and loose-limbed mover, which is why he indulges in his constant exercises on the field, stretching the groin and hamstring muscles to keep himself lithe. It is part of the man's total devotion to the game.

Derek Underwood, who has benefited so much from his liaison with Knott, remains completely entranced by his friend's dedication after nearly twenty years in the game:

Day in and day out he is the best in the world. No one gives himself so totally to the game. As soon as we arrive at the ground he is changed and ready for practice. We have to bowl to him to get his rhythm going and then he wants balls thrown to left and right so that he can practise diving, gently at first and then with increasing difficulty. As soon as the skipper has tossed up, it is more practice. Either more wicket-keeping routines or, if we are batting, he is round to the nets and practising in earnest. It doesn't matter whether we are playing at Lord's or Ashby de la Zouch, the routine is the same. Total dedication.

Nor is the dedication restricted to the field. Some ten years ago an American health expert advised him that if he wanted to obtain the maximum energy output, he should eat only natural foods. He has maintained a strict diet since that day. Meat and cheese are never eaten at the same meal. There must be no artificial preservatives. Tea is taken with honey, and food during a match will be mainly fruit and milk. He polishes his knife and fork before eating and maintains rigorous standards of hygiene. These are fads which have led many to call him a hypochondriac and suggest that he has begun to retreat into himself, but the man's record speaks for itself. He played ninety-five Tests without the slightest suggestion that he should be omitted, and it is quite likely that, but for Packer and South Africa, he could have played ninety-five more.

He is a private and inward-looking man who is conscious of the state of his own mind and body. He insists that his calisthenics and his Spartan-like discipline and dedication are the only things that have made it possible for him to survive at the top level. This thought and dedication are not solely concerned with his own mind and body, but also his equipment.

The red gloves to which he has given his name and which are now worn by more club cricketers than any other wicket-keeper's gloves, were determined after thought and trial. He wanted strong leather backs to the gloves as they help to keep the palm cups in position. Unlike Bob Taylor, he has no desire to 'feel' the ball and would like to take away all sensation of the ball hitting the glove and arrive at something akin to a baseball mitt. Each glove finger must have a rubber cap and the whole emphasis is on protection. He wears two pairs of inner gloves, which he does not dampen, and as well as taping the little fingers, he sometimes tapes a strip of sponge rubber to the inners along the base of his fingers. Like all keepers, he works at his gloves, pounding a cup between thumb, index and middle fingers.

He learned much from Les Ames, 'Hopper' Levett and Godfrey Evans, and the practitioners he admired most were Jimmy Binks and Keith Andrew, but essentially Alan Knott is an original. He is a genius who has fashioned keeping to his own art. He has inspired many, but none will ever be able to imitate him completely.

Allied to his brilliant wicket-keeping is batting of a very high quality which has brought 4389 runs, including five centuries and thirty 50s, most of them coming at a time when they were most desperately needed. He became the first wicket-keeper after Ames to score a hundred in an England *v*. Australia Test match.

As the years have passed, his batting has become increasingly unorthodox, so that his top hand is now so far round that the palm almost faces the bowler, and his stance has become more and more front on. His formidable powers of concentration are the basis of his batting, but he has an animal-like instinct for survival and a hawk-eyed vigilance. Neither does his batting lack flair, for his attacking willingness has turned the course of many a game.

When he went to the West Indies in 1967–8, the first of his six major tours, he was kept out of the first three Tests by Jim Parks, the selectors considering potential run-getting more important than first-rate wicket-keeping – a popular fallacy. Parks kept badly and failed with the bat. Knott played three innings in two Tests, was dismissed only once, and scored 149 runs. In the fifth Test he batted for the last 4 hours of the match to score 73 not out and save the game, and the rubber, for England. It was only his fourth Test match.

Four years later, after Massie had devastated England at Lord's, Knott gained revenge in the final Test at the Oval when he thrashed him violently, and often quite outrageously, in scoring an exhilarating 92. He was probably at his best against Lillee and Thomson, but his quick-footedness allowed him to defeat the Indian spinners on their home grounds. Cruelly, he was robbed of a maiden Test hundred in Karachi in March 1968 when rioters brought the match to an end with Knott on 96 not out. He finally got his hundred against Pakistan at Egdbaston in 1971.

After the Centenary Test he joined Kerry Packer's World Series Cricket, and when the South African Breweries recruited their rebel England team, he was one of the 'rebels'. Once more, his decisions were reached after profound thought. He is, by nature, not an optimistic man. He has worked unflinchingly to reach the highest summit of his profession, but he believes that the end could have come at any moment through injury or illness, which he has dreaded, or simply by loss of flair. He is essentially a family man and has taken every measure to provide for his wife and son; Packer and South Africa were part of those measures.

Perhaps the constant self-analysis has led him to be unsure of himself, but he believed that he could not rely on his natural ability to raise him to the highest level and so he cultivated patience and hard work. It was these two things that gave him his great powers of concentration.

He rarely makes a gesture that has not been considered. The busyness and swooping to left and right in between deliveries is all part of the fitness urge, the need to maintain flexibility and to relax, so that the next ball will be given the same concentration as the first of the day. He is meticulous in all that he does. Even his packing is deliberate and structured: the teddybear mascot is the last item before the lid is closed.

He has always felt that too much cricket is played in England. He stated some years ago that he would never tour again, and the reason that prompted that decision is the same one that may cause him to leave the game in the next few years – he wants more time with his wife and family.

When he does leave he will have imprinted on the minds of all who saw him an indelible image of quick movement, constant physical activity, eccentric exercises practised in solemn dedication, and leaping, darting, brilliant wicket-keeping which many say they have never seen equalled. He has transcended statistics. Merely to read the list of his catches, stumpings and runs is to learn nothing of the man's art.

He was bred of an age when the one-day game began to flourish and the wicket-keeper started to move back. He shaped and refined the lessons that Murray and Parks had given in this direction, but 'He would have been a great keeper in any age.'

16

Bob Taylor:
the Last of the Purists

If Murray, Parks and Knott had their keeping fashioned by the demands of the one-day game, then Bob Taylor is an anachronism. He is the wicket-keeper purist, the natural descendant of Bert Oldfield, from whom he used to obtain his gloves, and of Keith Andrew, whom he admires above all other keepers: 'Keith never seemed to miss a catch or a stumping. He was always behind the ball.'

Alan Knott said that he always wants to stand back in a limited-over game because it is so vital to prevent any byes: 'If you concede two lots of four byes, you can lose your side the match.'

Bob Taylor, on the other hand, believes differently:

The real test of a wicket-keeper comes when he has to show how good are his reactions, hands and anticipation when standing up. A lot of judges see this purely in relation to slow bowlers, but in my opinion it applies to medium-pacers and sometimes even fast bowlers.

On rare occasions, it's tactically necessary to stand up to the quickies; it happened with me in Pakistan when Javed Miandad was going down the wicket to John Lever and scuffing up the wicket deliberately so Pakistan's slow bowlers could take advantage of a worn wicket the next day. It was my biggest challenge of that tour, because John Lever's pretty sharp, and with his left-arm slant across the right-handed batsman I had to look nippy on many occasions, especially with the ball keeping so low. I was pleased with my performance because I caught Miandad when he chopped Lever down hard and I caught the under edge just outside the off stump.

Taylor maintained the practice of standing up to everything possible and practical in the one-day game. His attitude is the exact opposite of Alan Knott's: 'You should want to stand up to the medium-pace bowlers. It should be a matter of pride.'

When Taylor started with Derbyshire he kept wicket to the big, medium-paced in-swingers of Ian Buxton. Realizing that many batsmen play walking shots through mid-wicket (Les Ames remembers stumping Wally Hammond off 'Tich' Freeman off such an attempted shot), Taylor stood up to Buxton and stumped several batsmen off his bowling. He has continued the practice with Buxton's successors and frequently stands up to Tunnicliffe and Oldham after the first few overs with the new ball.

Taylor's beginnings as a wicket-keeper were different from those of Murray, Parks and Knott. Whereas many of the great wicket-keepers have adopted the position almost by accident, Taylor came to it by design and an appetite for the job. It has not diminished with the years. He recalls how it all started:

I was about eight or nine and when we used to play cricket I used to field on the boundary. Nobody ever hit the ball there and I got bored. When we played football I was centre forward and always in the game. I used to go and look at the notice board where the sportsmaster would put up the results of the matches and where my name would be underlined if I'd scored a goal. I liked that and I wanted to be in the action just as much at cricket, so I went to the sportsmaster and asked him if I could keep wicket. That was the beginning of my passion for the job and I have never lost it.

I used to play in the street and we used to play in the cinder car-park at Stoke City's football ground. When I was thirteen my sportsmaster took me to Bignall End Cricket Club and I played in the under-eighteen side. They were a fine club to me and I had some splendid coaching from Aaron Lockett and Jack Ikin. Neither of them had been wicket-keepers, but they taught me so much about concentration and the development of natural talent.

I went to watch Godfrey Evans at Old Trafford. He was

England's wicket-keeper at the time and my first hero. Then it was Keith Andrew. He was the supreme artist, quietly confident. I've never seen anyone to touch him.

There is much of Keith Andrew's wicket-keeping in Bob Taylor. Like Andrew, Taylor is neat and unspectacular. He is a striver after perfection and it is as important for him to perform without blemish before a handful of people on a chilly day at Derby as it is for him to accomplish great deeds in front of 20,000 spectators at Lord's. When he felt that his wicket-keeping was beginning to suffer he asked to be relieved of the captaincy of Derbyshire, although no one else had noticed a decline in his standards. Many people feel that, like Andrew, Taylor has been roughly treated.

He was playing for Bignall End in the North Staffs and South Cheshire League when he was fifteen and he played for Staffordshire in the Minor Counties before he was sixteen. Cliff Gladwin, the ex-England and Derbyshire medium-pace bowler, saw Taylor playing in the North Staffs League and recommended him to his old county. Derbyshire have been economic with wicket-keepers – only Harry Elliott and Dawkes, as well as Taylor, have kept regularly for them in the past sixty-five years. Taylor was enlisted as understudy to Dawkes, and when the latter, then at the veteran stage, suffered a knee injury in the match at Old Trafford in early June Taylor was called up as his replacement.

He played his first match against Sussex at Derby and Ken Suttle was his first victim. He caught Bell and Lenham in the second innings, but his most memorable contribution in the match was that he stayed for the last 15 minutes of the contest with Harold Rhodes to save the game. Rhodes was batting in suede shoes because of a pulled muscle and a septic toe. Taylor played in seventeen matches that season and *Wisden* wrote that, when Dawkes was injured, 'Taylor grasped the opportunity to show that he will be an adequate successor.'

Dawkes's knee trouble forced him to retire before the beginning of the next season and, at the age of twenty-one, Taylor had a regular place in the Derbyshire side. He was now recognized as a wicket-keeper of the highest potential.

In 1964 he suffered a football injury while playing with Port Vale and was unfit for the beginning of the cricket season. Laurie Johnson took over and performed creditably, so that Derbyshire were tempted to continue with him, primarily a batsman, as this would allow them to play an extra batsman in the side at the expense of the specialist wicket-keeper – 'the shape of things to come'. Johnson kept in the first eight matches, but there was strong press criticism and eventually Taylor was restored to the side. He considers that it taught him a lesson. He gave up football to concentrate on cricket, and from that day he has maintained a strict self-discipline in the matter of fitness.

His only other serious injury came in 1967 when, playing at Leicester at the beginning of August, he edged a ball from Jack Birkenshaw into his eye in the second innings and suffered a detached retina. He lay on his back for three weeks with his future career in doubt, but he had recovered well enough to begin the next season.

In 1963 he took ten catches against Hampshire at Chesterfield, and when he performed the same feat against India at Bombay in 1979–80, he became the first wicket-keeper to take ten catches in a match twice, although Rodney Marsh and Arnold Long have both taken eleven catches in a match.

Arnold Long was a great, thinking wicket-keeper who, but for the presence of Knott and Taylor, might have attained international honours. He served both Surrey and Sussex well for a number of years, and as captain of Sussex he did much to revitalize the club.

One should not dwell too long on statistics, but in Taylor's case they suggest that he has missed very little over the years. He is quick to admit when he lets a chance go begging, but others believe that he debits himself with misses that others would not even consider chances. A few years ago a Derbyshire committee member was complaining that the side was not doing well because they were missing so many chances behind the wicket. 'What, has Bob Taylor missed a few?' someone asked. The Derbyshire man looked at the speaker incredulously. 'Bob Taylor! Good God, no. He doesn't miss chances.'

By the early seventies he was accepted as the master craftsman. In the eyes of the purist he was the best wicket-keeper in the world, yet behind the stumps for England was Alan Knott. The debate raged on the respective merits of the two keepers and it can never be resolved to the satisfaction of all. With typical modesty and generosity, Taylor considers Knott to be England's best Test match keeper, with the perfect temperament for those great occasions, and in his list of all-time greats he places Knott second only to Keith Andrew. It was not, however, the Kent man's superior wicket-keeping ability which clinched the Test place ahead of Taylor, but his batting.

Taylor went to Australia and New Zealand in 1970–71 as Knott's understudy, although he was five years older than the Kent man. He did not play in a Test in Australia, but Ray Illingworth gave him the consolation of a Test cap in the first match in New Zealand. He did not play for England again for another six years.

He was invariably reserve to Knott, and on one occasion, in India in 1976–7, Roger Tolchard was sent on tour as deputy wicket-keeper although Taylor was told to stand by, for, if anything happened to Knott, he would be flown out to play in the Test matches. Finally, when Knott joined the Packer World Series in 1977, Taylor won his place as England's wicket-keeper. He was thirty-six years old and at last he acquired the status and prestige that his exceptional ability deserved.

He was England's wicket-keeper in Pakistan, New Zealand and, in 1978–9, Australia.

In the fifth Test match at Adelaide England were 132 for 6 in their second innings when Taylor joined Miller. He scored 97 as the pair added 135. It was a heroic innings and through it England clinched the series.

Taylor has always felt that his batting has been under-rated. He is capable of firm and resolute defence and, if

147

he lacks power, he has a wide variety of neat and stylish shots.

The England selectors have never quite believed that a man of forty can still have quite the same appetite and zest for the game as a younger man and, in spite of breaking the Test record in the Jubilee Test in India, Taylor was replaced by Knott for the home series with the West Indies in 1980, peace with Packer having been declared. Bairstow came in for the last Test and the ill-starred Centenary Test, and as Knott declined to tour again, Bairstow and Downton were the wicket-keepers who went to the West Indies with Ian Botham's side.

Paul Downton retained the position for the first Test against Australia in 1981, but this was English cricket at its lowest ebb and Taylor returned to keep brilliantly at Lord's. This was Botham's last match as captain and Brearley returned to lead England in that dramatic series, 'Phoenix from the Ashes'. It was now that Taylor was to suffer his cruellest treatment. Having kept splendidly in three Tests, he was dropped in favour of Knott. The specialist wicket-keeper was sacrificed because of the failing of front-line batsmen. He remained as cheerful and uncomplaining as ever: 'There are more than three hundred professional cricketers in the country and they can't all play for England. I'm grateful that because of cricket I have been to so many places and seen so many things. I've been lucky.' No man in the game is more loved.

He is a modest, dedicated man, devoted to his family and to his profession, and his long career has been in the very best traditions of the game.

He was back in the England side after that series, and although he was stupidly omitted from England's Prudential World Cup side when once more the insubstantial philosophy of selecting a moderate keeper who might scramble a few runs at number seven was adhered to. In a limited-over match the number-seven batsman should not be needed for more than a couple of overs. England paid the price for this nonsense.

In 1984 he went to Pakistan and New Zealand as

England's only wicket-keeper. It was his forty-third year and his twenty-second in first-class cricket, but his joy is undiminished.

One of his greatest moments was when Derbyshire won the Nat West Trophy in 1981, and, having lived through twenty years of less-than-palatial facilities at Derby, he would like to enjoy the magnificent new furnishings there for a few years before he leaves the game. Even then, he would like to keep close to cricket. He wants to help young wicket-keepers, for it is a field where coaching has been grossly inadequate.

He has practised relentlessly over the years. He believes that the promising young wicket-keeper should be a good fielder anywhere, for then he has the basic necessities of anticipation, agility and a good pair of hands. Once he goes behind the stumps he must develop concentration, for that is the key to success and the most difficult thing to acquire. In this respect, he admires Bruce French of Notts, who overcame personal problems and worked hard to acquire concentration. As Taylor says:

Concentration is everything. I am naturally right-handed, so I practise catching with my left hand every day in order to strengthen what was a weakness. I practise keeping wicket without the batsman there and in a match I am able to keep as if he did not exist and as if every ball was coming to me. The most difficult bowler to keep to is the off-spinner because the ball is always coming at you through the gate and for much of the time you are blind. I have been lucky here in that over the years I have kept to Geoff Miller and this has sharpened me.

I would advise all young keepers to work at their batting because so much emphasis is placed upon it these days, particularly in the one-day game. I told Andy Brassington he needed to improve his batting and it is only his weakness there that has cost him his place. He is a superb wicket-keeper and he's been very hard done by.

Like Knott, Taylor wears two pairs of inner gloves and does not dampen them. He likes to feel the ball and prefers a softer glove, which is why he first got his gloves from Bert Oldfield on the recommendation of Keith Andrew.

Also like Knott, Taylor is fastidious about his dress. The neckerchief and the white hat turned up at the back have become an essential part of his profile and if the hat falls off to reveal the grey hair, one is always surprised, for the movement of the man is essentially graceful and youthful.

There is a restrained effervescence about him. He is not flamboyant, but his enthusiasm bubbles over infectiously and he leaps in the air at the success of others as much as for his own success. Unfailingly kind and sociable, he was nicknamed 'Chat' by his England colleagues as a compliment to his skill in making conversation at the social gatherings that form a large part of any tour. His powers of persuasion can be seen in that he was able to convince England team-mates to divert a large part of their players' kitty to the cause of Mother Teresa in Calcutta. He is not an easy man to resist. He does everything as though he were doing it for the first time in his life. For him the world is a most exciting place.

When he finally retires to his home in Stoke, which he has named 'Hambledon' and which is as trim and tidy as one would expect from a man who gathers ragged throws from the outfield and makes them look as if they were really accurate, the world of cricket will be a duller place. He has given so much to it and taken so little in return.

Knott or Taylor? None will ever know the answer. Wasim Bari will say only this: 'When I came to England in 1967 the two best wicket-keepers were Knott and Taylor. When I came to England in 1983 the two best wicket-keepers were Knott and Taylor.'

17

'Old Iron Gloves':
Rodney Marsh

While Bob Taylor was dismissing more batsmen than any wicket-keeper had ever accounted for in a career, and building a combination with Ian Botham that was to become more prolific in terms of catches than any other similar combination in England's Test history, and while Alan Knott was moving relentlessly towards his Test records, Australia introduced into their Test side a left-handed batsman who kept wicket. His name is Rodney Marsh.

Few players in the history of the game excite more contrasting responses both from spectators and fellow players. When he last appeared in England, in the Prudential World Cup match against India at Chelmsford, he was booed on to the pitch for no apparent reason. When the team returned to Australia several players expressed the view that if Marsh had been captain, Australia could well have won the cup. When asked whom he considered to be the best international keeper he had ever played against, one Test player said vehemently, 'You don't expect me to say Rodney Marsh, do you?' Warren Lees and Wasim Bari, on the other hand, give Marsh the highest praise. 'Look at the man's record,' says Warren Lees passionately. 'You can't deny him that. He has the natural ability to catch. Nobody could have taught him to do that. He's marvellous.'

What is the man's record? He has played in ninety-one Test matches for Australia – a record. He has caught 322 batsmen and stumped 12 in those Tests, a total of 334 dismissals – a record. He has taken 88 catches off Dennis

Lillee in Test matches – a record. It is, as Warren Lees affirms, an achievement that cannot be dismissed lightly.

Rodney Marsh has had much to overcome. When he was chosen for Australia in the series against Illingworth's England team of 1970–71 the selection created much controversy. The general public had believed the tried, elegant and highly capable Brian Taber would retain the position and Marsh's selection caused a shock. A greater shock was to come when he was seen in action in his first Test, at Brisbane. He held four catches, but he seemed to drop the ball so many times that he won the nickname 'Iron Gloves'. He appeared fat and little more than a slip fielder in pads. He was clumsy and ungainly and he lumbered to collect returns from the field. Few could have believed when they saw him at Brisbane in November 1970 that he would play fifty-two consecutive matches for Australia and would then only lose his place because he chose to play for Kerry Packer's World Series Cricket.

Reared on Oldfield, Tallon and Grout, the Australian press and public considered Marsh to be the worst wicket-keeper ever to represent Australia. He was slow of reflex and ponderous of action, so that his selection seemed incomprehensible. Don Bradman and his selectors, however, were aware that cricket was moving into a new age in which the demands on a wicket-keeper were to be totally different from those that had been made of Oldfield and Ames. The emphasis had changed and was now centred on pace bowling, favoured by regular new balls, and the wicket-keeper would, henceforth, spend most of his time standing back. Marsh's few stumpings reflect this, but then, in the course of his Test career, he has kept to very few spinners. Gleeson, O'Keefe, Jenner, Mallett and Bright all played in Test sides along with Marsh, but, of these, only Mallett was really of the highest quality. Most of the time Marsh's keeping has been to Lillee, Thomson, Massie, Pascoe, Lawson, Hogg and the seemingly unending array of quick bowlers that Australia unearths.

Marsh was born in Armadale, Perth, in 1947, and it was for Armadale that he first kept wicket. He was in their under-sixteen team at the age of eight. He would practise cricket with his brother Graham, now a world-famous golfer, and from his earliest years he showed a strong combative attitude to the sport. He spent countless hours in the back-yard of his home, practising the techniques of wicket-keeping, so convinced was he that he was capable of reaching international level. It was a conviction he confided to his team-mate at Western Australia University Cricket Club, John Inverarity.

Marsh moved up through the grades and in 1968–9 he made his debut for Western Australia. It was against the West Indian touring team at Perth and he scored 104. Two years later he was in the Australian Test side.

He could not have been unaffected by the adverse criticism that he received in the press. His selection was due in some measure to Australia's search for middle-order batting after the dreadful drubbing that they had had in South Africa. This was the last Test series, from January to March 1970, in which South Africa took part before their excommunication from international cricket, and the home side won each of the four Tests by a considerable margin.

It was Ian Chappell who welcomed Marsh into the Australian camp and consoled him when Lawry declared in the fifth Test with Marsh on 92 not out. Lawry was to play only one more Test and then Ian Chappell took over. Dennis Lillee had made his debut in the previous Test and a great era had begun for Australian cricket.

Stung by the comments about him in that first Test series, Marsh realized that he was neither fit enough nor fast enough for international cricket, and that part of his problem was that he was carrying too much weight. He has always enjoyed good living, but he maintained a careful diet so that where once he was described as fat, now he was referred to as strong and muscular. His short legs were totally unsuited for running, but he set himself some punishing tasks on hilly terrain near his home in Perth and the result of his training programme was that he became very quick over a short distance. When Ian Chappell led the Australian side to England in 1972

Marsh was a fitter and more capable keeper. He took England by surprise with a record 23 dismissals in the series, 2 of them stumped, and 242 runs, an average of 34.57.

In the first Test he equalled an Australian wicket-keeping record with five catches in an innings and, with defeat imminent, he hit a glorious 91 in 123 minutes with four mighty 6s off Gifford. As a keeper, he distinguished himself throughout the tour, flinging himself in all directions to collect some wild deliveries from Lillee.

He and Lillee had played together since Marsh was a trainee teacher who also played for the Western Australia University Club and Lillee played for the Perth Club. He had kept to Lillee in all the fast bowler's Tests and in the majority of the state games, too. It has been a lethal combination, rewarded when both men became record holders as bowler and wicket-keeper for their country. They have an understanding born of deep respect for each other and it has brought some memorable achievements.

In a Gillette Cup semi-final against Queensland, Western Australia defended a miserable score of 77, and won. The crucial point of their victory was when Greg Chappell was caught behind third ball. Marsh indicated to Lillee that he wanted a bouncer down the leg-side. Chappell swung it away, supposedly for 4, but Marsh had stationed himself some 4 yards wide on the leg-side and plucked the ball out of the air. His trust in his friend's bowling abilities has been unwavering.

Marsh became the first Australian wicket-keeper to score a Test hundred when he hit 118 against Pakistan in the first Test of 1972–3. In addition he scored a career-best 236 against them for Western Australia the same season. He also hit a hundred against New Zealand and played what was probably his best innings when he scored 110 not out in the Centenary Test at Melbourne.

He is a forceful, belligerent hitter of the ball, with a powerful straight drive and a ferocious cut. He exudes aggression as he bludgeons bowlers to all parts of the field, but it is true to say that his batting skills have diminished in the past six years. The same cannot be said of his ability as a wicket-keeper.

His dedication to training has been maintained. He accepted the necessity to stand back deep to Lillee and Thomson, to give himself a wider arc of vision and a larger area in which to operate for his diving, tumbling catches. He practises diving to left and right consistently. Team-mates are cajoled into hitting balls hard to his left and right, and Marsh launches himself, like a swimmer diving at the start of a race, and takes the ball, mostly one-handed, before he crashes to earth where the landing, too, must be effected properly so that the catch is not jolted loose. No keeper in the history of the game has taken wide catches so regularly, and it was this 'width' that gave Ian Chappell's team of the seventies an extra fielding dimension.

It is not always appreciated that in the thin air of Australia the ball has a habit of dipping and swerving after it has passed the bat, but Marsh adapted to all conditions. There have been few others more dedicated in turning themselves into top-class players, and there has been none tougher. Ames and Levett do not think Marsh as versatile as Knott, but they consider him a great wicket-keeper in his own style, with magnificent footwork to the quick bowlers which marks him as of the very highest class.

It is the toughness which is the essence of the character. There is a neatness about him which is at variance with the open shirt revealing a hairy chest, the bandit moustache bristling aggression, and the cap barely covering the shaggy hair and worn in a jaunty, almost arrogant manner. The aggression, the arrogance and the raucous appeal of Marsh epitomized the fierce Australian side of the seventies. He was a natural lieutenant to Ian Chappell.

Records tumbled over each other as his career progressed. He had 26 catches against the West Indies in 1975–6 and 11 catches in the Sheffield Shield game against Victoria the same season. In the next season there were 10 catches in the match against South Australia at

Perth. No wicket-keeper in Test history has had five victims in an innings as many times. The nickname 'Iron Gloves' is now remembered only with affection. He has long since changed it to the 'Iron Man'.

He joined World Series Cricket to double his income from the game and so become a full-time professional cricketer. Few relished the 'circus' matches more than he, but then, he has never done anything by halves. He has continued to be a fervent upholder of Kerry Packer's action in forming the pirate Test series, and he has maintained that he played some of the hardest cricket of his life for the Packer organization.

Many thought that his career would be at an end when World Series Cricket was disbanded, but he returned to the official game with renewed vigour, and achieved further records. He has lasted an abnormally long time in the game by modern Australian standards and, at the age of thirty-six, he has shown no sign of relinquishing his place as Australia's top wicket-keeper.

There were times when his aggressive approach on the field lost the respect of the crowd, and there were reports that violent reactions off the field to what he considered unjust decisions on it strained the nerves and patience of county clubs in England, yet socially few men are more charming.

Sponsors in England have not always been as well repaid by touring sides or counties as they might have been, but Marsh has never failed to attend functions when requested and to make sure that his host's social gathering was a success. 'It is to Marsh that we owe the success that this after-match party has become every year,' said one organizer gratefully.

None plays it harder and with more unquenchable spirit. None has worked harder to reach the top. He has scaled every height that was there to be scaled by an Australian cricketer. Only one peak remains unreached – the Australian captaincy. And there are many who believe that he may well reach that summit before he leaves the game.

18

Wasim Bari and the Commonwealth Tradition

The length of time that England, Australia and South Africa were engaged in international cricket before the West Indies, New Zealand, India, Pakistan and Sri Lanka became Test-playing nations gave them the opportunity to establish traditions in wicket-keeping which are only now being shaped by the others. Wicket-keeping is a tradition, an instinctive art which is passed on from generation to generation and moulded by the demands of the time. Rodney Marsh has said that he learned most about wicket-keeping from watching Alan Knott.

Before the war New Zealand had Ken James, who played for Northamptonshire between 1935 and 1939. He was one of the first to stand back to medium-pace bowling, but he also kept splendidly to the leg-breaks of Bill Merritt. He was a man who enjoyed the game immensely, and in gesture he anticipated John Murray. In a memorable game between the Army and the RAF at Lord's in 1943 he caught the first four army batsmen in a space of 23 deliveries from Austin Matthews.

In 1968 New Zealand found her greatest wicket-keeper in Ken Wadsworth. He was, like Warren Lees, who had the unenviable task of succeeding him, totally uncoached and reached the very highest standard solely through dedication. He had a pugnacity, a desire to win that had not been too prevalent among his colleagues, and his influence upon New Zealand cricket was profound. His last innings in an international match was 46 not out in 47 minutes against India in a limited-over game at Auckland during February 1976, in which he stumped Gaekwad.

Six months later he died of cancer at the age of twenty-nine.

With their concentration on speed, the West Indies have tended to look for reliable catchers rather than outstanding wicket-keepers and Jeff Dujon, a batsman first and a wicket-keeper almost by default, falls into that category. His predecessor, Deryck Murray, played in sixty-two Tests and was a strongly influential member of some great West Indian teams. He was a steady and generally reliable keeper who was at times fortunate to retain his place in the Test side and who never touched the heights of effervescent brilliance associated with the greatest wicket-keepers.

It is difficult for a wicket-keeper to develop his art if he is standing back all the time and, conversely, he is more able to acquire the necessary skills if he is asked to keep to high-quality spin bowling. It is for this reason that the Indian sub-continent has been quicker to produce wicket-keepers of the very highest standard than other countries.

When Les Ames visited Pakistan as manager of the MCC under-twenty-five team in 1967 he expressed the view that he had seen the best wicket-keeper to have come out of the Indian sub-continent. He was referring to an eighteen-year-old student named Wasim Bari. So impressive was Bari that he was sent to England with Hanif Mohammad's side and played in all three Tests. *Wisden* greeted him with acclaim: 'As a wicket-keeper, Wasim Bari was almost infallible, taking his chances without fuss.' It was the beginning of a Test career that has so far lasted seventeen years. If dedication and enthusiasm have any influence on the longevity of a career, Bari's Test career will last for at least another seventeen years.

He believes that the length of wicket-keeping careers is due to an inborn, God-given gift. Without this innate gift, which Ames, Oldfield and Knott all discovered they had, it's not possible to be a wicket-keeper, but it is a gift that needs to be worked at, and dedication and concentration are essential if a wicket-keeper is to cultivate the gift that has been accorded him.

Bari speaks with reverence of his profession. He pulsates with the joy of life: 'You must forgive me if I seem to be staring at you. I have become so used to staring fixedly at the ball that it now seems that I stare at people.' His eyes twinkle with fun, but he is serious. He continues: 'I wanted to play cricket for Pakistan from the time that I was very young. I saw that my way to the Pakistan team was as a wicket-keeper and since I first kept wicket I have never wanted to do anything else. I do not mind where I bat, or if I bat, as long as they allow me to keep wicket.'

The sense of dedication and enthusiasm was with him from the start. He knew Godfrey Evans to have been one of the greatest of wicket-keepers and one of whom he had heard legendary tales. He read all that Evans had written and when he came to England he met the man himself and has continued to meet him over the years. He is always ready to learn.

He had read of Hammond's great ability as a cricketer and although he had never seen him, he had an admiration for him. He read Hammond's books and learned that one must never be stationary, one must be always active in the game.

'Observe and learn,' he says. 'That is the only way to become a wicket-keeper, and after seventeen years I am still doing it.'

From the start, Bari's wicket-keeping was neat and calm. He is 5 feet 9 inches tall, beautifully balanced and extremely agile. He is acrobatic in that he has taken some thrilling diving catches when standing back to pace-bowlers like Imran Khan and Sarfraz Nawaz, but his strength in this direction lies in the fact that he is an expert judge of when it is necessary for a wicket-keeper to dive. He will fling himself and take the catch only if he assesses that the ball will not reach the slips. Bob Taylor reckons that he has no equal in his ability to judge in this way.

While accepting that the true judgement of a keeper is how he performs standing up to the spinners, Bari tells of the delight of keeping to bowlers of real pace: 'I would love to have kept to Lillee and Thomson and to the West Indian fast bowlers. It is a great challenge and demands acrobatic skills. Leeds in 1971 was a real joy. That was when I took eight catches against England; some of them were diving and sprawling in front of first slip. That was my most exciting match.'

Bari went from strength to strength on that tour and his eight catches in the final Test equalled the Test record. He established a new world record in the first New Zealand innings at Auckland in 1979 when he caught seven of the first eight batsmen.

He sees his task as a constant challenge which keeps him fresh:

In the past few years Imran has developed late in-swingers with the old ball. He is very quick and he swings the ball yards, so that keeping wicket to him has become physically harder.

The one-day game has presented a new challenge, too. Batting, bowling and wicket-keeping are all different. It is necessary to concentrate even more than you do in a Test match, if that is possible, but the whole game is so much more concentrated and you have the feeling that every run is crucial.

His lowest point as a keeper was in 1977 and 1978 when he captained Pakistan against England. This was an uneasy period for Pakistan when their side, decimated by the Packer controversy, was inexperienced and unsettled. He led them with commendable calm, but his wicket-keeping suffered. 'I do not think I was a captain,' he says. 'I found it a distraction from my wicket-keeping.' But there is no hint of complaint.

Later, the Pakistan selectors tried to replace him behind the stumps, but no one could rival him in safeness and consistency. He has now overtaken Majid Khan and with seventy-six Test appearances is the most capped player in Pakistan Test history.

He is sympathetic to his rivals: 'It is hard keeping wicket in Pakistan and India. The ball keeps low all the time and it is a miserable life for a wicket-keeper because he is down all the time. You get the advantage of keeping to many spinners, but it is still very hard work.' The keeping to spin, of course, is revealed in the dismissals. In half the number of Tests that Knott had played, Bari had the same number of stumpings.

The advent of Abdul Qadir in the last three years has also meant a boost, as Bari explains: 'He gained confidence and I gained confidence in keeping to him. He bowls two different types of googly, which not everyone realizes. He has made me a better keeper. Look – he gave me five dismissals in the World Cup, two catches and three stumpings. He is good for me.'

His judgement of keepers is based on their durability: 'After ten years of Tests in different countries, only then can you really tell how good a wicket-keeper is.' This is why he rates Knott and Taylor above others and why he talks to them about their art. His earliest admiration was for Wally Grout.

Nothing has changed for him over the years: the joy is still there. He sat on the dressing room balcony at the Oval during the Prudential World Cup semi-final against the West Indies in 1983, and said: 'After sixteen years of Test cricket this still seems like my first match to me. I am excited about every game that I play. I have never understood any other way. If God allowed me to have my life again and I went back twenty-five or twenty-six years, I would still want to keep wicket for Pakistan.'

He reads much, but he believes that cricket is the best education in helping one to learn how to be a good human being.

He wishes to continue as long as possible in the game that he loves. At thirty-six he feels he needs more rest – which is why he was granted permission by the Pakistan Board not to play in the Quaid-e-Azam domestic competition in 1982–3 – and even greater determination. Does he strive for perfection? He shakes his head. 'I read in America a book by Khalil Gibran, in which he said, "To become a perfectionist you have to become God's shadow, which is impossible." '

It is possible that Wasim Bari will not become a perfectionist, but he will remain one of the world's great wicket-keepers and he has certainly become a very good human being.

19

In the Shadow of Engineer: Syed Kirmani

An equally good human being is Wasim Bari's counter-part in the Indian team, Syed Mutjaba Hussain Kirmani. He is a year younger than Bari and his way to the top has been more littered with obstacles, and therefore slower.

The first wicket-keeper that Kirmani saw was Kunderan, in 1966, when he was seventeen years old and was selected for the Indian Schools' side. There were five wicket-keepers in the side and Kirmani was chosen as a batsman. He responded by topping the averages.

Kunderan himself had been a product of India's mass coaching scheme, and he encouraged the young players. He played in eighteen Tests, sometimes as a batsman, once as a bowler, but most frequently as a wicket-keeper. In the first Test against England in 1961–2 he established an Indian record by catching three and stumping two of the eight English wickets that fell in the first innings. He was replaced by Engineer for the next match.

It was Engineer who was to stand in the way of Kirmani and immediate recognition. When India toured the West Indies in 1970–71 Pollamani Krishnamurthy kept in all five Tests and gained a reputation for standing up close to even the fastest bowlers. It was Krishnamurthy and Kirmani who came to England later that season, but neither of them played, for Engineer, who was under contract to Lancashire, was released to play in the Test matches.

Farokh Engineer was a dashing character. He kept wicket with enthusiasm and brashness, and lifted an Indian side which could easily slip into lethargy on the field. He was sound but flamboyant as a keeper, and there was a stylish unorthodoxy about him. Accomplished as he was as a wicket-keeper, Engineer is best remembered as a personality with aggressive and confident batting that made him immensely popular with Lancashire and, indeed, wherever he played.

His flamboyance and his bright batting tended to over-shadow the quieter Kirmani, who came to England again in 1974 as Engineer's understudy, topped the batting averages, had the most dismissals on the tour, and once more did not play in a Test. He was back again the next year for the first World Cup, but did not play a game.

After his success as a batsman with the Indian Schools' side Kirmani had kept wicket in the nets. Provision was made for wicket-keepers to display their talents and it was in the nets that he took the eye and received the approbation and encouragement of Kunderan.

When he came to England in 1971 Kirmani was most impressed by Knott and Taylor. He watched them and spoke to them. Knott, in particular, gave him much advice on fitness and practice, as Kirmani recalls:

A wicket-keeper is born and not made. You are born with anticipation, good reflexes and the power to develop sound judgement, but I had to work hard at catching practice. Prac-tise, practise, practise is what I have always done, because only with constant practice and exercise will you arrive at the level of anticipation necessary on the field. I have had to work hard, too, to maintain physical fitness. Alan Knott has taught me much about this and I do many back-stretching and knee exercises.

Kirmani has been lucky in the variety of the Indian attack in recent years, for, where once there was only spin, now there is Kapil Dev's pace and the medium wiles of Madan Lal.

Warren Lees, an able keeper, who started his career as an opening bowler and then became a wicket-keeper, at the age of ten, has the greatest admiration for Kirmani. He considers him, along with Taylor, the great artist,

Knott and Marsh, the supreme catcher, to be the greatest of Test wicket-keepers.

Lees maintains:

The most difficult thing in Test cricket is the last half hour of any day. The concentration has to be so intense that by the end of the day you are beginning to wilt, whether you are batting or keeping wicket. To see Kirmani keeping to Chandrasekhar throughout a long, very hot day, and see him as sharp at the end as he was at the beginning was a revelation. We found it hard enough to bat against him. Goodness knows what he was like to keep wicket to.

Kirmani says that the part of wicket-keeping he enjoys most is taking difficult bowlers, and it was Chandrasekhar, with his zestful googlies and leg-breaks, who gave him the greatest challenge and the greatest pleasure:

It is all a matter of judgement on the field and you have more time to make a judgement when you are standing back than when you are standing up. This is what makes the sharpness in taking bowlers like Chandrasekhar necessary and why you must keep fit. Standing back, the demands are different, and that is where Rodney Marsh is so good. He stops and catches anything when standing back. In the one-day game that has become vital. The pressures on a wicket-keeper in World Cup matches are very great because a mistake could cost a bye which could lose the match. Another thing that people do not understand is how difficult it is for a wicket-keeper to adjust to different wickets. They talk of the difficulties for the batsman, but it is the same for the wicket-keeper.

When Engineer retired in 1976 Kirmani had no rival for the job as India's wicket-keeper. He played his first Test in Auckland in January 1976, and although he was without a dismissal in that match, he had five catches and a stumping in the New Zealand innings in the second Test to establish an Indian record and equal the then world Test record. Those were his first dismissals on the way to becoming the first Indian wicket-keeper to claim 100 victims in Test cricket, a mark he reached in his forty-second Test. By the summer of 1983 he had increased his total to 137 in fifty-eight Tests, so that Engineer's 82 in forty-six Tests has long since been left behind. Only Oldfield and Evans among the Test centurions have a higher proportion of stumpings.

Kirmani's record would have been even more impressive but for the fact that his rumoured association with the Packer organization cost him his place on the 1979 tour to England and his place in the side for the World Cup the same year. He was sorely missed and his return to the side for the Test series against Australia in 1979–80 was welcomed by all.

The greatest triumph lay ahead: his magnificent wicket-keeping and courageous batting was a force in India's triumph in the Prudential World Cup of 1983. He had 12 catches and 2 stumpings in the competition, and the catches in the semi-final to dismiss Gower and in the final to account for Bacchus, were memorable.

A year earlier in England Kirmani had made a deep impression on the younger keepers who were seeing him in action for the first time. He combines a calm assurance with a sparkling zest for the job. His shaven head and his bright, stylish keeping have established him as a personality in world cricket. Like Bob Taylor, his long journey in the wilderness has made the ultimate accolade even sweeter.

He remains essentially a purist as a wicket-keeper. In spite of the century of dismissals in Test cricket, his most satisfying accomplishment in his own mind is that he did not concede a bye in three successive Test matches against Keith Fletcher's side in 1981–2. He loves standing behind the stumps, but he thinks it is a thankless job. Few appreciate the skill or the difficulty. There is little encouragement. Perhaps the real encouragement and thanks come from the young players he has influenced, who, like David East of Essex, say, 'What a keeper! I didn't realize he was as good as that!'

20

Conclusion

Time present and time past
Are both perhaps present in time future. . . .

Certainly Eliot's lines, though not intended, are relevant
to the art of wicket-keeping. It is, as already noted, a
tradition that is passed on, shaped by its times and its
practitioners.

Paul Downton, already a Test player, learned much
from Alan Knott in his days with Kent. The great man
taught him about catching the ball two-handed, and when
he watched Marsh and Dujon he saw that what Knottie
had said was right. He has played for two great counties
and has had the advantage of keeping to Underwood,
Emburey and Edmonds, and, in doing so, he has gained
in rhythm and balance, the rudiments of which he learned
from Knott.

Now, Downton has the problem of dealing with Phil
Edmonds's full length and big drift, but he finds these
easier to cope with than the occasional bowling of Mike
Gatting, an enthusiastic bowler who moves the ball, but
is a little wayward.

As Wasim Bari said: 'Observe and learn.'

'I learned something from watching Kirmani,' says
Paul Downton. 'He is such a good mover, so supple, and,
above all, completely unflappable.'

Jack Richards says that the hardest thing, when one
first starts, is concentration:

I was only fourteen when I kept for Penzance Cricket Club, and a year later I was in the Cornwall under-fifteen side. I used to be as interested in horse riding as I was in cricket, but cricket took over. I played in the Minor Counties, travelled in the west and joined Surrey.

Naturally, you are very keen when you start, and you don't lose the enthusiasm; but it gets hard. It is very hard to keep the concentration when you first come into the three-day game. You need a new sense of commitment and it has to be worked at, and you are always learning.

I watched Knottie. He's the all-action keeper, all movement. And I watched Bob Taylor. His movement is minimal. Everything is easy. You learn something from both of them, but in the end you have to sort out your own way.

I was lucky in that I had Intikhab to keep to when I started, and that was an education. And Pat Pocock, like any off-spinner, gives you problems; but there are problems with the pace-men, too, that you have to sort out. With Sylvester Clarke, you must be prepared to have to go very wide to take the ball, but at the same time to be looking for the one that is going to come straight through.

Concentration is the vital thing. A bye can mean a lost bonus point or even defeat in a one-day game, yet at the same time, you have got to pressurize the batsman by standing up.

I still think that the work of the wicket-keeper is undervalued. What is involved is not understood by many people.

Paul Downton, Jack Richards, Bobby Parks, David East – a young and exciting generation of keepers to carry on a great tradition. Downton has had two tours and played for England at home and abroad. Richards has played in one-day internationals. Parks, neat, tidy and courteous in all he does, is a wicket-keeper by inclination and passion, whereas his father was one by accident. East is in the Evans mould – bounding enthusiasm, a dynamic zest for the game and an unquenchable spirit, allied to outstanding ability.

What is to be hoped is that their talents will be recognized by those who administer the game, and that there will be a greater sensitivity to the value and skill of the man behind the stumps. He gives so much to the game and, perhaps like all givers, is taken too much for granted.

LEADING WICKET-KEEPERS AND THEIR RECORDS

FIRST CLASS	CAREER	INNS.	NOs	RUNS	H.S.	AVERAGE	100s	TOTAL DISM.	CT.	ST.
Ames, L. E. G.	1926–51	950	95	37245	295	43.56	102	1113	698	415
Andrew, K. V.	1952–66	476	160	4230	76	13.38		905	721	184
Bairstow, D. L.	1970–	482	92	9498	145	24.35	4	840	731	109
Barnett, B. A.	1929–61			5531		27.51	3	358	216	142
Binks, J. G.	1955–75	598	129	6910	95	14.73		1071	895	176
Blackham, J. M.	1874–94	442	61	6395	109	16.78	1	451	272	179
Booth, R.	1951–70	671	134	10138	113*	18.87	2	1122	946	176
Brown, G.	1908–33	1012	52	25649	232*	26.71	37	596	528	68
Butt, H. R.	1890–1912			7313		12.94		1262	971	291
Cameron, H. B.	1924–35	161	17	5396	182	37.47	11	224	155	69
Carter, H.	1898–1921			2897		19.98	2	273	186	87
Cornford, W. L.	1921–47			6327		14.61		1000	656	344
Dolphin, A.	1905–27			4191		10.76		719	488	231
Downton, P. R.	1977–	160	28	2437	90*	18.46		347	305	42
Duckworth, G.	1923–47	544	195	4932	75	14.13		1090	751	339
East, D. E.	1981–	81	15	1304	91	19.75		168	149	19
Engineer, F. M.	1958–76	510	55	13436	192	29.52	13	824	703	121
Evans, T. G.	1939–69	753	52	14882	144	21.22	7	1060	811	249
Farrimond, W.	1924–39			2656		22.32		336	256	80
Grout, A. T. W.	1946–66	253	24	5168	119	22.57	4	588	473	115
Halliwell, E. A.	1891–1909			1702		19.34		101	69	32
Huish, F. H.	1895–1914							1328	952	376
Hunter, D.	1889–1909							1327	955	372
James, K. C.	1923–47	330	41	6413	109*	22.19	7	418	310	108
Jarman, B. N.	1955–69			5615		20.00	5	560	431	129
Jones, E. W.	1961–	591	119	8341	146*	17.67	3	933	840	93
Kelly, J. J.	1894–1907			4106		19.83	3	355	242	113
Kirmani, S. M. H.	1967–	277	52	5924	116	26.32	3	360	171	89
Knott, A. P. E.	1964–	699	127	17431	156	30.47	17	1260	1129	131

Langley, G. R. A.	1945–67			3236		25.68	369	4	293	76
Lees, W. K.	1970–	184	32	3616	152	23.78	235	4	207	28
Levett, W. H. V.	1930–47			2524		12.25	467		272	195
Lilley, A. F. A.	1891–1911	639	46	15591	171	26.29	899	16	709	190
Lindsay, D. T.	1958–73	214	15	7074	216	35.54	333	12	293	40
Long, A.	1960–80	537	131	6801	92	16.75	1046		922	124
Marsh, R. W.	1968–	379	37	10607	236	31.01	810	11	750	60
McIntyre, A. J. W.	1938–63	567	79	11145	143*	22.83	797	7	639	158
Murray, D. A.	1971–	161	27	4200	206*	31.34	289	7	258	31
Murray, D. L.	1961–82	566	87	13640	166*	28.41	837	10	729	108
Murray, J. T.	1952–75	939	136	18872	142	23.50	1526	16	1268	258
Oldfield, W. A. S.	1919–38	315	57	6135	137	23.77	661	6	400	261
Parks, J. M.	1949–76	1227	172	36673	205*	34.76	1182	51	1089	93
Parks, R. J.	1980–	87	18	1093	64*	15.84	205		182	23
Pilling, R.	1877–89			2696		9.91	597		417	180
Richards, C. J.	1976–	197	46	3214	117*	21.28	341	1	303	38
Sherwell, P. W.	1902–13			1808		29.10	119	3	67	52
Smith, A. C.	1958–74	612	85	11027	145	20.92	771	3	710	61
Smith, E. J.	1904–30	814	55	16997	177	22.39	878	20	722	156
Spooner, R. T.	1948–59	580	72	13851	168*	27.26	765	12	585	180
Storer, W.	1887–1905	490	41	12966	216*	28.87	410	17	357	53
Street, G. B.	1909–23			4031		17.22	419	1	304	115
Strudwick, H.	1902–27	835	243	6445	93	10.89	1493		1235	258
Taber, H. B.	1964–74			2648		18.01	395	1	345	50
Tallon, D.	1933–54	228	21	6034	193	29.14	432	9	303	129
Taylor, B.	1949–73	949	73	19094	135	21.79	1294	9	1082	212
Taylor, R. W.	1961–	843	159	11521	100	16.84	1594	1	1424	170
Waite, J. H. B.	1948–65			9812		35.04	510	23	427	83
Wadsworth, K. J.	1968–76	164	23	3600	117	25.53	282	2	256	26
Wasim Bari	1964–	343	89	5530	177	21.77	786	2	641	145
Yarnold, H.	1938–55			3741		10.45	695		462	233

LEADING WICKET-KEEPERS AND THEIR RECORDS

TEST MATCHES	PLAYED	INNS.	NOs	RUNS	H.S.	AVERAGE	100s	TOTAL DISM.	CT.	ST.
Ames, L. E. G.	47	72	12	2434	149	40.56	8	98	75	23
Andrew, K. V.	2	4	1	29	15	9.66		1	1	
Bairstow, D. L.	4	7	1	125	59	20.83		13	12	1
Barnett, B. A.	4	8	1	195	57	27.85		5	3	2
Binks, J. G.	2	4		91	55	22.75		8	8	
Blackham, J. M.	35	62	11	800	74	15.68		60	36	24
Booth, R.										
Brown, G.	7	12	2	299	84	29.90		12	9	3
Butt, H. R.	3	4	1	22	13	7.33		2	1	1
Cameron, H. B.	26	45	4	1239	90	30.21		51	39	12
Carter, H.	28	46	8	873	72	22.97		65	44	21
Cornford, W. L.	4	4		36	18	9.00		8	5	3
Dolphin, A.	1	2		1	1	0.50		1	1	
Downton, P. R.	4	7	1	59	26*	9.83		8	8	
Duckworth, G.	24	28	12	234	39*	14.62		60	45	15
East, D. E.										
Engineer, F. M.	46	86	3	2611	121	31.08	2	82	66	16
Evans, T. G.	91	133	14	2439	104	20.49	2	219	173	46
Farrimond, W.	4	7		116	35	16.57		7	5	2
Grout, A. T. W.	51	67	8	890	74	15.00		187	163	24
Halliwell, E. A.	8	15		188	57	12.53		11	9	2
Huish, F. H.										
Hunter, D.										
James, K. C.	11	13	2	52	14	4.72		16	11	5
Jarman, B. N.	19	30	3	400	78	14.81		54	50	4
Jones, E. W.										
Kelly, J. J.	36	56	17	664	46*	17.02		63	43	20
Kirmani, S. M. H.	69	99	14	2100	101*	24.70	1	160	128	32
Knott, A. P. E.	95	149	15	4389	135	32.75	5	269	250	19

Name										
Langley, G. R. A.	20	37	12	33	374	14.96		98	83	15
Lees, W. K.	21	37	4	152	778	23.57	1	64	57	7
Levett, W. H. V.	1	2	1	5*	7	7.00		3	3	
Lilley, A. F. A.	35	52	8	84	903	20.52		92	70	22
Lindsay, D. T.	19	31	1	182	1130	37.66	3	59	57	2
Long, A.										
Marsh, R. W.	91	144	11	132	3558	26.75	3	334	322	12
McIntyre, A. J. W.	3	6		7	19	3.16		8	8	
Murray, D. A.	19	31	3	84	601	21.46		62	57	5
Murray, D. L.	62	96	9	91	1993	22.90		189	181	8
Murray, J. T.	21	28	5	112	506	22.00	1	55	52	3
Oldfield, W. A. S.	54	80	17	65*	1427	22.65		130	78	52
Parks, J. M.	46	68	7	108*	1962	32.16	2	114	103	11
Parks, R. J.										
Pilling, R.	8	13	1	23	91	7.58		14	10	4
Richards, C. J.										
Sherwell, P. W.	13	22	4	115	427	23.72	1	36	20	16
Smith, A. C.	6	7	3	69*	118	29.50		20	20	
Smith, E. J.	11	14	1	22	113	8.69		20	17	3
Spooner, R. T.	7	14	1	92	354	27.23		12	10	2
Storer, W.	6	11		51	215	19.54		11	11	
Street, G. B.	1	2	1	7*	11	11.00		1		1
Strudwick, H.	28	42	13	24	230	7.93		72	60	12
Taber, H. B.	16	27	5	48	353	16.04		60	56	4
Tallon, D.	21	26	3	92	394	17.13		58	50	8
Taylor, B.										
Taylor, R. W.	51	74	12	97	1073	17.30		162	155	7
Waite, J. H. B.	50	86	7	134	2405	30.44	4	141	124	17
Wadsworth, K. J.	33	51	4	80	1010	21.48		96	92	4
Wasim Bari	73	102	24	85	1259	16.14		201	175	26
Yarnold, H.										

The columns showing total dismissals and catches include catches taken in the field

Index

Abdul Qadir, 161
Accrington, 24
Alexander, F. C. M., 94, 125
Allen, D., 125
Allen, G. O., 50, 70, 79, 86, 90
Altham, H. S., 24, 28, 30
Ames, L. E. G., 24, 25, 63, 73, 77–91, 95, 115–16, 118, 125, 137, 140, 144, 152, 155, 158
Andrew, K., 72, 73, 122–3, 129–30, 143–7, 150
Archer, R., 107
Armadale, 152–3
Armstrong, W., 47, 59
Arsenal FC, 126
Ashton, C. T., 90
Australian Imperial Forces, 63, 65–6

Bacchus, S. F. A., 165
Bailey, T. E., 115–18, 120
Bairstow, D. L., 10, 148
Bakewell, A. H., 96
Balaskas, X., 95
Barclay's World of Cricket, 52
Bardsley, W., 46, 60, 65, 101
Barnado, Dr, 76
Barnes, S. F., 46–8, 58
Barnes, S. G., 104
Barnett, B. A., 70
Barnett, C. J., 70
Barrington, K., 125

Beauclerk, Lord Frederick, 19
Beckenham CC, 65
Bedford, 74
Bedser, A. V., 85, 117
Bell, A. J., 96
Bell, R. V., 145
Belvedere, 137
Benaud, R., 14, 105, 108, 110
Bennett, Arnold, 121
Beslee, 83
Bignall End CC, 144–5
Binks, J., 128–31, 140
Bird, Albert, 44
Birkenshaw, J., 146
Birmingham, 35, 43
Blackham, J.Mc., 24–33, 43, 98
Blackheath, 84, 115
Bligh, Hon. E., 19
Blythe, C., 84
Booth, R., 87, 125
Bosanquet, B., 38–9
Botham, I. T., 148, 151
Bournville, 35, 43–8
Bowes, W. E., 90
Box, T., 21–3
Boycott, G., 14, 52, 111
Bradman, D. G., 12, 70, 77–8, 87, 100–9, 118, 152
Brassington, A., 149
Braund, L., 54
Brearley, J. M., 52, 134, 137, 148
Brearley, W., 32, 77
Brentford FC, 126
Brentwood, 74, 90
Brett, 18
Briggs, J., 30

Bright, R. J., 152
Brighton College, 74
Broadbridge, 20
Brockwell, 30
Brown, F. R., 104
Brown, George, 50, 58–9, 60
Brown, W. A., 102
Brown of Brighton, 20
Buckston, R. H. R., 116
Budd, 20
Buller, S., 133
Bundaberg, 99–100
Burge, P., 105
Buxton, I., 144

Cadbury Bros., 35
Calthorpe, Hon. F. S. G., 49, 74
Cameron, H. B., 93–8
Canterbury, 90, 121
Carbine, 31
Cardus, Neville, 53, 58, 60, 73, 75, 76, 78
Carlton CC, 25
Carr, A. W., 50, 60
Carr, D. W., 40
Carter, H. S., 24, 66–7
Catt, A., 137
Chandrasekhar, B., 164
Chapman, A. P. F., 60, 67, 77
Chappell, G. S., 154
Chappell, I. M., 153–5
Chipperfield, A. G., 88
Clark, E. W., 88
Clarke, S. T., 167
Clarke, W., 22
Clayton, G., 136
Clift, P., 25
Clode, 56

Close, D. B., 132
Coldwell, L., 130
Collins, H. L., 65–6
Compton, D. C. S., 103, 117, 119, 127, 131
Compton, L. H., 127
Constantine, L., 87
Conway, J., 26
Cornford, J., 74
Cornford, W. 'Tich', 73–4
Cornwall, 167
Cowdrey, M. C., 123, 130, 132
Cowie, J., 102
Cox, G., 74
Crawford, J. N., 55
Crump, B., 122
Cutmore, J., 90

Darling, J., 29
Davidson, A., 110
Davies, H. G., 116
Dawkes, G., 145
Denison, W., 19, 21
Denton, D., 41
Derbyshire CCC, 37, 49, 50, 115–16, 143–50
Dexter, E. R., 91, 128–9
Dixon, A., 136
Dodds, T. C., 74
Dollery, H. E., 51
Dolphin, A., 45, 58–9
Douglas, J. W. H. T., 45–6, 48, 58
Dover, 87, 116
Downton, P. R., 10, 34, 78, 135, 148, 166–7
Duckworth, G., 24, 59, 73–80, 85, 89
Duff, R. A., 38
Dujon, P. J., 158, 166
Durston, J., 115

East, D. E., 86, 133, 165, 167
East Moseley, 65
Eastbourne, 59
Edmonds, P. H., 166
Edrich, J. H., 111
Edrich, W. J., 119
Edwards, G. N., 89
Eliot, T. S., 166
Elliott, H., 75, 145
Emburey, J. E., 166

Emmett, G. M., 103
Engineer, F., 162–5
Essex CCC, 56
Evans, D. L., 25
Evans, T. G., 22, 61, 80, 90, 105, 109, 113–24, 127–8, 136–8, 140, 144–5, 159, 165, 167

Fagg, A., 90
Farrimond, W., 78–9, 89
Faulkner, A., 93
Fingleton, J. H., 69, 103–5
Fitzgerald, R. A., 9
Fleetwood-Smith, L., 69, 70
Fletcher, K. W. R., 165
Folkestone, 83, 87, 89
Ford, 30
Foster, F. R., 40–2, 44–5, 50–1
Fowler, A., 126
Fox, 12
Freeman, A. P., 12, 13, 67, 82–5, 90, 144
French, B., 149
Frith, D., 61

Gaekwad, A. E., 157
Gatting, M. W., 166
Geary, G., 50
Gentlemen v. Players, 20, 21, 22, 45, 57, 75, 87, 90
Gibb, P. A., 116
Giffen, G., 27, 29, 30
Gifford, N., 154
Gilbert, E. A., 100
Gilbey's, 121
Gilligan, A. E. R., 50, 67, 73
Gilligan, A. H. H., 74
Gillingham, 91
Gladwin, C., 145
Glamorgan CCC, 25, 108, 134
Glebe CC, 64
Gleeson, J. W., 152
Gloucestershire CCC, 42, 48, 87, 103, 126
Goddard, T. W., 85, 90
Gould, I. J., 10
Gower, D. I., 34, 60, 165

Graburn, W. C., 55
Grace, Dr W. G., 26, 27, 28, 36, 37, 44, 55
Graveney, T. W., 117, 132
Gravesend, 115
Greenough, T., 114
Greensmith, W., 97
Gregory, D. W., 27
Gregory, J. M., 65–9, 101
Gregory, S., 29–30, 64
Griffith, C., 132
Griffith, S. C., 60, 74, 116, 120
Grimmett, C. V., 63, 69
Grout, A. W. T., 108–12, 114, 128, 133, 152, 160
Gunn, G., 66
Gupte, 114

Hall, W., 110, 125
Halliwell, E., 92–3, 98
Hambledon, 17, 18
Hammond, J., 19
Hammond, W. R., 13, 71, 78, 87–90, 95–6, 102, 116, 159
Hampshire CCC, 49, 97, 146
Hanif Mohammad, 158
Harding, N., 116
Hargreave, S., 44
Harris, Lord, 28, 30
Hartigan, G., 48
Harvey, R. N., 105, 115
Hassett, A. L., 105
Hawke, Lord, 30
Hawke, N., 110, 111
Hayes, F. C., 134
Hayman, Francis, 15
Hayward, T., 35, 45, 93
Hearn, 82
Hearne, J. W., 66
Heath, Capt., 58
Hendren, E. P., 84–7
Hendry, H. L., 71
Hever, 82
Higgins, J. B., 83
Hill, C., 40, 46–7
Hirst, G., 38
Hitch, 66
Hobbs, J. B., 12, 46, 55, 56, 62, 66–8, 73
Hogarth, William, 15

Hogg, R. M., 152
Hollies, W. E., 118
Hornby, 27
Horsfall, 74
Howell, H., 49
Hubble, J. C., 80, 82, 83
Huish, F., 45, 56, 80, 84
Hulme (Derbyshire), 37
Hunte, C., 125
Hutton, L., 70, 103, 104, 107, 122
Hythe, 82

Ikin, J. T., 144
Illingworth, R., 121, 125, 147, 152
Imran Khan, 159
Inglewood, 28
Intikhab Alam, 167
Inverarity, R. J., 153
Iremonger, 46
Iverson, J., 104

James, K. C., 157
Jardine, D. R., 45, 84
Jarman, B., 109
Jarvis, 29
Javed Miandad, 143
Jenner, T., 152
Jenner-Fust, 20–2, 80
Jennings, R. V., 98
Jessop, G., 51
Johnson, I. W., 102–3, 106
Johnson, L., 146
Johnston, B., 13–14, 73, 110, 138
Jones, E. W., 24, 25, 122, 133
Jupp, 27
Jupp, V. W. C., 84

Kanhai, R., 89
Kapil Dev, R. N., 163
Kelleway, C., 63–7
Kelly, J. J., 32–3, 39–40, 66
Kent CCC, 11, 17, 20, 23, 43, 59, 80–91, 114–21, 136–42, 147
Kenyon, D., 118
Khalil Gibran, 161
Kilner, 50
King (Leicestershire), 58
Kinneir, 46

Kirmani, S. M. H., 162–6
Kline, L., 110
Knight, A. E., 9–10
Knight, G. T., 20, 22
Knott, A. P. E., 13, 24, 57, 80, 121, 133–4, 136–51, 155, 157–60, 163, 166, 167
Knox, 77
Kortright, C., 37, 77
Kotze, J. J., 92
Krishnamurthy, P., 162
Kunderan, B. K., 162–3

Ladbrooke's, 121
Laker, J. C., 14, 85, 118
Lambert, 19
Lancashire CCC, 24, 74–9, 116, 123, 134, 136, 163
Langley, G., 105–8
Langridge, James, 90, 95
Langridge, John, 13
Larwood, Harold, 50, 69, 72, 86, 90, 94, 100
Lawry, W., 130, 153
Lawson, G. F., 152
Lawton, T., 126
Leer, G., 18–19
Lees, W. K., 56, 151–2, 157, 163–4
Leicestershire CCC, 9, 58, 136, 146
Lenham, L., 145
Lever, J. K., 143
Leveson-Gower, H. D. G., 57, 60, 62, 95
Levett, W. H. V., 10–13, 80–1, 91, 113, 115, 119, 129, 140, 155
Lewis, A. R., 34, 113
Lewis, C., 137
Lewis, J., 34
Leyland, M., 96
Liddicutt, 66
Lillee, D. K., 141, 151–3, 160
Lilley, A. F. A. 'Dick', 24, 34–45, 51–2, 57, 92–3, 98
Lillywhite, James, 20, 26
Lillywhite, John, 23

Lindsay, D., 97–8, 109, 133
Lindwall, R. R., 102, 108, 110
Lockwood, 30, 56
Lockyer, T., 23
London County XI, 44, 55
Long, A., 146
Long, E., 65
Lyons, 30
Lyttleton, Hon. A., 29
Lyttleton, Hon. E., 24, 28

Macartney, C., 68
Macaulay, G., 50
McCool, C., 102, 117
McDonald, E. A., 67, 74–6, 84
MacGregor, G., 37
McIntyre, A., 84–5
Mackay, K., 110
McKenzie, G., 110
MacLaren, A. C., 29, 35, 59
Madan Lal, S., 163
Maddocks, L., 107, 109
Maidwell, 11
Mailey, A. A., 60, 63, 67
Majid Khan, 159
Mallett, A., 152
Marlar, R. G., 124
Marner, P., 136
Marriott, C. S., 88
Marsh, G., 153
Marsh, R. W., 97, 146, 151–7, 164, 166
Marshall, John, 76, 79
Marshall, M. D., 26
Marshall (Surrey), 56
Martyn, H., 76, 80
Massie, R., 141, 152
Matthews, A. D. G., 157
May, P. B. H., 105, 107, 122–3
MCC, 9, 15, 16, 27, 32, 50, 79, 91, 100, 123
Mead, C. P., 66, 84
Meckiff, I., 110
Merritt, W., 157
Merton CC, 65
Meyer, B., 133
Middlesex CCC, 22, 28, 65, 90–1, 126–36

Miller, G., 147, 149
Miller, K. R., 102, 117
Millman, G., 128–9
Mitcham, 53, 62
Mitchell, T. B., 95
Morris, A. R., 105, 118
Morris, W. B., 74, 122
Mullery, A., 127
Murdoch, W. L., 26–9
Murphy, P., 46
Murray, D. L., 131, 158
Murray, J. T., 10, 109, 124–36, 142–4, 157
Mynn, A., 20

Nash, M., 14
New South Wales, 32, 33, 66, 101, 105, 130
Nichols, M. S., 88, 95
Noble, M. A., 59
Norfolk, Duke of, 129
North Middlesex CC, 65
Northamptonshire CCC, 87, 122–3
Nottinghamshire CCC, 22, 50, 83, 91
Nupen, 96
Nyren, John, 9, 16–19

Oakes, C., 74
O'Keefe, K., 152
Oldfield, W. A., 24, 25, 52, 61, 63–73, 76–7, 80, 86–7, 95, 98–9, 102, 106, 108, 119, 143, 150, 152, 158, 165
Oldham, S., 144
O'Reilly, W. J., 63, 70, 102, 118
O'Shea, T., 99–100
Oxenham, R. K., 100
Oxford University, 54, 65
Oxford v. Cambridge, 21

Packer, K., 140–2, 147, 152, 157, 159, 165
Parker, C., 84
Parkin, C., 74
Parks, J. M., 123–35, 141–4
Parks, R. J., 86, 167
Parsons, J. H., 49

Pascoe, L. S., 152
Pawson, A. G., 54, 82
Pawson, A. H., 82, 90
Pawson, P., 126
Pearce, T. N., 74, 90
Peel, R., 30
Penzance CC, 167
Perth CC, 154
Pilling, R., 24–5
Pinder, 23
Plumb, 23
Plymouth Argyle FC, 137
Pocock, P. I., 167
Pogson, N., 33
Ponsford, W. H., 60, 78, 100
Pooley, E., 23, 26–7, 101
Poon, H., 100
Pope, D. F., 90
Port Vale FC, 146
Potter, 20
Povey, 82
Price, W. F., 101
Prittie, Hon. T. C. F., 11
Pycroft, Rev. James, 20

Quaife, W. G., 41
Queensland, 66, 99–106, 109–12, 130, 154
Quiddington, 19

Ramadhin, K. T., 125
Randall, D. W., 34
Ranjitsinhji, K. S., 9, 10, 39
Ransford, V. J., 46–7
Rees, 134
Rhodes, H., 145
Rhodes, W., 40, 48
Richards, C. J., 86, 166–7
Richardson, T., 30, 36, 56, 57
Richardson, V., 101, 107
Robertson-Glasgow, R. C., 71
Robins, D. H., 134
Robinson, D. C., 48
Root, F., 50
Rorke, G., 110
Rugby Boys' Club, 126
Rushby, 56–7

Ryder, J., 67–8
Ryder, R., 52

Saggers, R., 107
St John's Ambulance Brigade, 49
Sarfraz Nawaz, 159
Schwartz, R., 93
Selassie, Emperor Haile, 72
Selby, 27
Sharp, H., 115
Shaw, Alfred, 26–8
Shaw, G. B., 88
Sheppard, Rev. D. S., 129
Sherwell, P., 92–3, 98
Sherwin, M., 24
Shilton, 35
Siggs, D., 109
Silk, D. R., 127
Simpson, G., 119
Simpson, R., 110
Simpson-Hayward, G. H., 57
Sims, J., 126
Small, J., 17
Smeeth CC, 81–2
Smethwick, 35
Smith, A. C., 129–30
Smith, C. I. J., 90
Smith, E. J. 'Tiger', 40–52, 58, 63, 66, 70, 101
Smith, H., 43
Smith, H. (Gloucester), 75
Smith, M. J. K., 111, 132
Smith, 'Razor', 57–8
Smith, T. P. B., 117
Somerset CCC, 54, 94, 97, 110–11, 136
South African Breweries, 141
South Australia, 100, 155
South Melbourne, 26
Southampton, 83
Spofforth, F. R., 24, 26
Statham, J. B., 125
Stedman, F., 55–6
Stevens, 'Lumpy', 17
Stockport, 28
Stoddart, A. E., 36
Stoke City FC, 144

INDEX

Storer, W., 36–7
Street, G., 59, 73
Strudwick, H., 40, 45–8, 50, 53–63, 66, 73, 75, 84, 98, 107, 126, 134
Sturt CC, 107
Sueter, T., 17–19
Surrey CCC, 23, 53–4, 55, 56–8, 60, 61, 66, 84, 101, 115, 146, 167
Sussex CCC, 19, 22, 49, 101, 145–6
Sutcliffe, H., 12, 53, 84, 100
Sutcliffe, W. H. H., 117
Suttle, K., 145
Swetman, R., 121–5
Sydney Sun, 78
Sydney University, 26

Taber, B., 97, 152
Tallon, D., 99–108, 114, 117, 152
Tallon, L. W., 99
Tancred, 44
Tate, F. W., 40
Tate, M. W., 50, 60, 73, 84
Taylor, Brian, 123–4
Taylor, Derek, 110–11
Taylor, J. M., 66
Taylor, K., 121
Taylor, R. M., 90
Taylor, R. W., 10, 24, 72, 122, 134, 140, 143–51, 159, 160, 163, 165, 167
Tennyson, L. H., 49, 66, 93
Teresa, Mother, 150
Thomson, J. R., 141, 152–5, 160
Titmus, F. J., 111, 127, 134
Tobin, 100

Tolchard, R. W., 10, 135, 147
Tonbridge, 82, 87
Toowoomba, 100
Toshack, E., 102
Triangular Tournament, 47
Tribe, G., 102
Trott, A., 57
Trueman, F. S., 125
Trumble, H., 32, 39, 40
Trumper, V., 40
Tunbridge Wells, 11, 12, 83
Tunnicliffe, C. J., 144
Tyldesley, E., 84
Tyldesley, J. T., 55
Tylecote, E., 24, 80
Tyson, F., 122

Ufton, D., 137
Underwood, D. L., 121, 138–9

Valentine, B. H., 90
Vaughton, H., 48
Verity, H., 95
Vernon, 28
Victoria, 26, 29, 32, 33, 66, 99, 100, 155
Vine, J., 46
Vogler, A., 93

Wade, H. F., 94
Wadsworth, K., 157–8
Waite, J., 97–8
Walcott, C., 89, 125
Walker, C. W., 70
Warner, P. F., 22, 42, 45, 46, 47, 89, 98
Warrington, 74
Warwickshire CCC, 35, 40–4, 48–51, 56, 82, 87, 130

Wasim Bari, 109, 150, 151, 158–62, 166
Watson, 125
Watt, A. E., 90
Wattle CC, 65
Wazir Ali, S., 79
Webb, R., 124
Weigall, G., 82
Wellard, A. W., 90
Wenman, E. G., 19–22, 80
Wensley, A. F., 73
Western Australia, 153–6
Westminster Gazette, 42
White, 93
Whysall, 59, 67, 75
Wickham, Rev. A., 96–7
Willes, J., 19
Willsher, E., 23
Wilson, A., 126
Wilson, Miss, 53–4
Wood, D., 74
Wood, G. E. C., 59, 80
Woodfull, W. M., 69, 78
Woolley, F. E., 13, 40, 50, 66, 67, 83, 84, 88
Woolmer, R. A., 91, 138
Worcestershire CCC, 12, 39, 44, 83, 94, 125
Wordsworth, C., 21
Worrell, F., 133
Wright, D. V. P., 90, 117
Wyatt, R. E. S., 77–8, 96

Yalden, W., 17, 19
Yarnold, H., 124–5
Yorkshire CCC, 28, 41–2, 121, 124, 131

Zulfiqar Ahmed, 108